Daniel Harris
8T

TOUGHER THAN EVER – the official inside story of TV's biggest challenge

DAN WADDELL

THIS IS A CARLTON BOOK

Text copyright © Carlton Books Limited 2002
Pictures © John Rogers/Carlton Television 2002
Design copyright © Carlton Books Limited 2002

This edition published in 2002 by Carlton Books Limited
An imprint of the Carlton Publishing Group
20 Mortimer Street
London
W1T 3JW

A CIP catalogue for this book is available from the British
Library.

ISBN 1 84222 668 1

Cover design: Alison Tutton
Design: Penny Dawes
Production: Janette Burgin

Contents

acknowledgements

I would like to thank all 12 contestants for giving up their time to be interviewed and answering my questions honestly and thoughtfully. I also extend my thanks to the '13th' Survivor, Beverley Mansell, who agreed to be interviewed for this book despite her disappointment, and last year's winner Charlotte Hobrough.

At Planet 24 I am indebted to Ed Forsdick who was incredibly helpful, both in Panama and back in London. Despite the pressure he was under and the workload he had to contend with, he was unfailingly cheerful – well, almost – and took time to answer queries, allow me access to contestants and video footage with good grace and humour throughout. Cheers Ed. I must also offer a hearty slap on the back to Kevin Reid who, despite thrashing me at pool in the 'Loop' bar did more to help than he had any right to. His dedication to *Survivor* almost matches his dedication to Celtic. The logistics of staging such a huge production mean that any additional problems are a nuisance, especially pasty-faced book authors with last-minute demands for boats, planes and aspirin. Fortunately for me, the production team were a joy to work with: thanks to Christina Sayers, Debi Roach, Jo Wallett, Jane Macauley, Beccy Green, Louise Thomas, Emma Curtis and Iain Wimbush. You made my job extremely easy. I must also make special mention here of

Chris Sussman, the esteemed author of the Treemails, for his help. Other sources of invaluable information were Jill Robinson and her team of producers, Simon Tucker, Mark Nicholas and Stephen Flett. Once back in London I was safe in the capable hands of Alice Bartley and Alice Denny who fielded all my inquiries with their usual good humour.

Deserving a paragraph of their own are the team whose transcriptions are essential for a project such as this. Without the skills of Angela Parker, Kelly-Ann McHale, Paul 'Biggie' Evans and Ellie Hardy this book would have been impossible.

I would like to thank Penny Simpson at Carlton Books for commissioning this project and being such fun to work with again; my agent Araminta Whitley and her assistant Celia Hayley; 'Jungle' John Rogers for his excellent photographic work and for being a conscientious roommate and Nick Lockett and John Manthorpe at Carlton who, once again, proved invaluable.

In no particular order, I would also like to thank: Peter Johnston, Debbie Stammers, Silvana Job, Annie Gillott, Ben Woodgate, Chris Brogden, Iain Andrews, Nick Gottschalk, Duncan Gaudin, Gary Brooks, Steve Blincoe, Simon Quinn, Dave Marriott, Vince Doyle, Neil Purcell, Simon Llewellyn Graham Johnson, Mark Owen, Mark McCafferty, Andrew Thurgood, Mark Dawes and Hash Shalaan. If I have missed out anyone at all then I apologise.

Finally, I owe more thanks than I can recount here to my wife, Emma.

timeline

Day 1	Arrive on North and South islands
Day 2	Build camps
Day 3	Immunity Challenge: Assault Course
Day 4	Sarah voted off
Day 5	Reward Challenge: Canoe Rescue
Day 6	Immunity Challenge: Hanging Around
Day 7	Lee voted off
Day 8	Reward Challenge: Fire and Ice
Day 9	Immunity Challenge: Swimming Relay
Day 10	Tayfun voted off
Day 11	Reward Challenge: Ambassador's Visit
Day 12	Immunity Challenge: Bug-eating
Day 13	Meeta voted off
Day 14	Home video
Day 15	Merger
Day 16	Reward Challenge: Breath Holding

Day 17   Special Tribal Council

Day 18   Reward Challenge: Broken Spears

Day 19   Immunity Challenge: Log Stand

Day 20   Helen voted off

Day 21   Reward Challenge: Spider Hunt

Day 22   Immunity Challenge: Obstacle Quiz

Day 23   Alastair voted off

Day 24   Reward Challenge: Balancing Beams

Day 25   Immunity Challenge: Ever Decreasing Targets

Day 26   Drew voted off

Day 27   Reward Challenge: Hands Up

Day 28   Immunity Challenge: Family Values

Day 29   Dave voted off

Day 30   Reward Challenge: Weight Guessing

Day 31   Immunity Challenge: Orientation Island

Day 32   Bridget voted off

Day 33   Reward Challenge: Fallen Comrades

Day 34   Immunity Challenge: Time's Up

Day 35   John voted off

Day 36   Rest Day

Day 37   Final Tribal Council

 North Island

Name: **Drew Agger**

Age: 27

DOB: 20.01.74

Occupation: Firefighter

Hometown: Hereford

Height: 5ft 9in

Weight: 9st 7lbs

Marital Status: Boyfriend Robin

Luxury Item: Photo of Robin

Qualifications: 8 GCSEs, business and financial diploma

Name: **Dave Porter**

Age: 55

DOB: 02.01.47

Occupation: Retired firefighter

Hometown: Newcastle

Height: 5ft 10in

Weight: 14st

Marital Status: Wife Rita; two sons

Luxury Item: Football

Qualifications: "All-round good egg"

Name: **Meeta Bose**

Age: 35

DOB: 29.09.66

Occupation: Financial Planning Manager

Hometown: Herts

Height: 5ft 7in

Weight: 11st

Marital Status: Partner Sonny

Luxury Item: Book about Reggie Kray

Qualifications: Chartered Institute of Bankers
    CESA, 1, 2 and 3

Name: **Tayfun Kadioglu**

Age: 27

DOB: 01.03.74

Occupation: Professional Competitive Latin
    American Dancer

Hometown: London

Height: 5ft 9in

Weight: 11st

Marital Status: Single

Luxury Item: Goggles

Qualifications: BA (Cantab), Maths and Management
Studies (1:1); three A-Levels at Grade A;
11 GCSEs at Grade A

Name: **Helen Carney**

Age: 22

DOB: 08.10.79

Occupation: Barmaid

Hometown: Sheffield

Height: 5ft 8in

Weight: 9st 7lbs

Marital Status: Single

Luxury Item: Hammock

Qualifications: BA Hons in Tourism, Recreation and
Leisure Management; City and Guilds in
Outdoor Activity Management

Name: **Alastair Brogan**

Age: 35

DOB: 12.04.67

Occupation: MD of a fuel distribution company

Hometown: Motherwell

Height: 6ft 4in

Weight: 16st

Marital Status: Single

Luxury Item: Frisbee

Qualifications: BA Sports and Recreation Management

Name: **Jonny Gibb**

Age: 31

DOB: 23.11.70

Occupation: Detective Constable

Hometown: Edinburgh

Height: 6ft

Weight: 13st 12lb

Marital Status: Girlfriend Ruth

Luxury Item: Inflatable couch

Qualifications: 7 O-Levels, three Highers

Name: **John Dalzell**

Age: 32

DOB: 23.11.69

Occupation: Barrister

Hometown: Winchester

Height: 5ft 5in

Weight: 10st

Marital Status: Girlfriend Mary

Luxury Item: Photo of Mary

Qualifications: Three A-Levels; BCE Hons; Law Diploma

Name: **Susannah Moffat**

Age: 27

DOB: 28.04.74

Occupation: English teacher

Hometown: London

Height: 5ft 11in

Weight: 10st 12lbs

Marital Status: Husband Barney

Luxury Item: Complete Works of Shakespeare

Qualifications: Three A-levels; BA Hons
        English Literature; PGCE

Name: **Sarah McCombie**

Age: 22

DOB: 05.08.79

Occupation: Broking Assistant

Hometown: London

Height: 5ft 9in

Weight: 9st 7lbs

Marital Status: Single

Luxury Item: Vaseline

Qualifications: Nine GCSEs; three A-levels

Name: **Lee Capon**

Age: 25

DOB: 24.05.76

Occupation: Area Aftersales Manager

Hometown: Benfleet, Essex

Height: 5ft 11in

Weight: 13st 10lbs

Marital Status: Single

Luxury Item: Lilo

Qualifications: 10 GCSEs; Customer Service NVQ;
Management NVQ

Name: **Bridget Griffiths**

Age: 43

DOB: 07.09.58

Occupation: Shepherdess

Hometown: Farringdon, Oxon

Height: 5ft ½in

Weight: 9st 5lbs

Marital Status: Divorced; two daughters; boyfriend John

Luxury Item: Boules

Qualifications: Clean driving licence

The Dirty Dozen

At first, Drew Agger was afraid. Actually, she was petrified. At 5pm on the evening before the second series of *Survivor* was to begin, she had just been informed that she would be appearing in the programme. As the series editor, Ed Forsdick, told her the news, her stomach lurched. A few weeks before she had not even been a reserve; she had sent a Christmas card to Planet 24 to thank them for considering her for the programme and asking them to keep her in mind should they find her suitable for any further productions. She believed that was the last she would hear of *Survivor*. But then in the New Year, Ed called to ask if she would be a reserve, the first choice having pulled out. Drew seized the chance but never imagined it would lead to a role in the show. Still, she negotiated six weeks' leave from her job as a firefighter, packed her bags and off she went. At least it would be a bit of a holiday, all expenses paid. Then on the eve of the game, as she watched TV in her hotel room, came the knock, followed by the shock. She had little time to consider the consequences, however, because 30 minutes later she was being ushered in to a meeting room at the El Panama Hotel in Panama City for a briefing, along with her fellow contestants.

Drew's last minute insertion was because of the withdrawal of Beverley Mansell. Initially, Beverley was to be a member of South Island, alongside Susannah Moffat, Lee Capon, Jonny Gibb, John Dalzell and Sarah McCombie. Bridget Griffiths was supposed to be a member of North Island, but Beverley's decision to return disrupted the carefully thought-out balance between the two groups. It was decided to switch Bridget to South Island and put Drew in North. Beverley was desperately disappointed to miss out on this chance of a lifetime, but her reasons were clear.

Beverley, a 45-year-old mother of three, was rendered speechless when she was told she had been selected to take part in *Survivor*. It was, she admits, an "opportunity of a lifetime". As a lover of the outdoor life, she had always been interested in the idea of being marooned on a desert island. Immediately, she threw herself in to preparing for island life, improving her swimming, memorising survival techniques, even working out in the adventure playground where she took her six-year-old son Grant. She became single-minded, focused on what lay ahead, planning every detail. She believes, however, that she may have focused too much on the challenge ahead, because a week or two before she was due to depart for Panama she began to notice small changes in Grant's behaviour. She had told him that her work teaching drama would take her overseas for six weeks and when she took him along to her drama classes she noticed a difference in the way he acted towards her, he seemed to afford her less respect than usual and appeared angry. When the camera crew came to film her at home, he made life difficult for her. She realised that she may not have taken into account the emotional effect on her young son.

She tried to explain to him, by showing him when she would return on a calendar, but where do you start explaining such an absence to a six-year-old boy? To him, six weeks seemed like forever. But she had the support of her adult daughter and son and her husband was happy to take care of Grant. She knew she would miss him tremendously but felt this was a chance she could not turn down. But over the next week his mood deteriorated. On the day she was due to leave, she took him home from school at dinnertime but he refused to eat his lunch. She told him about the airport and that she would be back in six weeks to meet him and his Dad. "But I want to pick you up now," he said. It was heartbreaking for Beverley but, encouraged by her daughter, she decided to go through with it, hoping Grant would come to accept her absence. That evening she flew down to London after an emotional farewell. She could think of little but her son and how her husband would cope. Not being able to tell other family members or friends about where she was really going was also tough because it made it difficult to ask for a helping hand.

Beverley called home the next day. She had always been there for her family but now she felt she wasn't able to look after them. The pull she felt was dreadful but she decided to go for it, promising to call when her flight from Heathrow landed in Miami. But the connection for the flight to Panama gave her no time to call and it was not until she reached her hotel in Panama City that she was able to do so. As it was 3am in the UK she was only able to leave a message, her voice tired and croaky. Such was her worry, she could not sleep, neither could she eat. The next day she knew she had to make a decision: either to stay and go through with it or return home to her family. The conflict was paralysing. After another day of being unable to eat or sleep and agonising over what she should do, on the Thursday morning she asked herself, "What on earth am

I doing?" Fretting about what would happen at home in her absence and worried that it might scar Grant emotionally, she was beginning to doubt her involvement. She had already rung to speak to a member of the Planet 24 team about her doubts when her phone rang: it was her husband. He said he had been worried by the sound of her voice on the message. When asked how Grant was, he responded that he was not doing so well; he had not eaten since she left and had been very quiet. He was obviously missing her desperately. Her husband urged her to go ahead but her mind was already being made up: a million pounds and the chance to go on the programme were not any-where near as valuable as her son and his wellbeing. Being on the island for six weeks without knowing how he was would be too much to bear. She spoke to Kevin Reid of Planet 24 and then to psychologist Stephen Flett. As she explained her predicament to him, her husband phoned once more. He said he thought he could cope for a week, maybe two, but six weeks was too long. There and then she took the final, wrenching decision to quit the show. The series editor Ed Forsdick came to see her, just a few hours before the briefing on the eve of the game, and she explained her reasons. He was, she said, "absolutely brilliant" and sympathetic to her plight.

"It was the one of the biggest decisions of my life," she says now. "I have massive regrets but it was also a massive relief to get home and find that everything was OK. If there was some way my husband and Grant could have flown out to Panama and been nearby should something have happened, so I could have got to them, even if it meant leaving the game, then that would have been all right. But being so far away was the problem; not knowing how he was would have been awful. It was not worth the risk." It was a shame, though a very under-standable decision: there are things far more important than TV shows and £1m prizes. There is no doubt that Beverley would

have fully appreciated her time on the island. It is certainly difficult to imagine her whinging about any aspect of island life or a
change in the game's rules. A few days after the game started, on
the first available flight, she returned to England and her family.

As Beverley came to terms with her decision, the 12
survivors came face to face at the briefing. It was not the first
time they had seen each other as some had been on the same
flight out of London. Though forbidden to speak to each other,
some of the more observant and curious survivors had already
spotted potential rivals and tribe mates. The most flagrant was
Tayfun Kadioglu, a flamboyant Latin-American competitive
dancer from London. Lee Capon, who immediately marked
Tayfun down as a fellow contestant, spotted him at Gatwick. "He
was already playing the game at the airport," adds Lee. Little did
he know. Tayfun, first to check in, said he was a member of a
party and could he find out where the rest of the group were?
While the survivors were all travelling under false names, Tayfun
managed to discover the seat numbers of each person on his
flight and made sure he got a good look at them all. Had his ruse
been discovered, he would have been in for an almighty dressing down – but then he would get one of those soon enough. A
bag of nervous energy, on the flight he grinned, winked and
fidgeted all the way to Panama, and was consequently noticed
by everyone else. Others were also making up their minds about
people they had seen on the flight, in particular Alastair Brogan,
who at 6 feet 4 inches looked every bit the part.

But the briefing was the first occasion on which all 12 had
set eyes on each other. In a corner, a lone camera filmed what
took place. They had to remain silent, which was difficult for the
more garrulous, like Dave. "We sat there for hours – it was worse
than a doctor's surgery. I'll talk to anybody, me – I'm not
bothered who it is. And I was looking around and everyone's
trying to avoid looking at each other or saying anything. So I

counted all the wall lights, the entire ceiling lights. There were 28 ceiling lights with two out, and eight wall lights with one out if I remember rightly. I was so bored. The silence was unbelievable."

Once everyone was assembled, Ed gave a talk, followed by a local guide, Paki, who gave them information about the inherent dangers they could face and what to do to avoid them. Then medic Dr Graham Johnson of Remote Trauma took them through the health hazards they may encounter, paying particular attention to the fact that more people die in the tropics after being hit by a falling coconut than they do from being bitten by an insect, snake or any other of the island's more predatory denizens. Few listened to what was being said, taking more time to study each other, and make eye contact. Sarah McCombie made an instant impression when she entered the room wearing a backless, fluorescent lime-green top. While some, such as Helen Carney and Drew, sought simply to seek reassurance in the eyes of the other contestants, the more ambitious started to size up the opposition. Detective Jonny Gibb noticed Alastair – who couldn't? – and John Dalzell, who despite his diminutive size looked fit and determined. Obviously ex-forces, thought Jonny. The only other person to catch his eye was a tall woman with curly brown hair, whom he assumed to be a doctor or a lawyer. It was Susannah Moffat, a 27-year-old schoolteacher. "I don't what it was about her but she just stood out. She just looked … very ambitious," he says.

After the briefing, all twelve were sent back to their hotels for a second night of confinement in Panama City. Each was visited by Ed Forsdick who asked if they were OK and understood the rules. To each, he repeated starkly, "If you smuggle anything on to the island then you will be disqualified." It was warning heeded by all – with a notable exception.

Back in her room Drew felt hideously unprepared, mentally and physically. Despite only having known she was in the game for a couple of hours, she was still better prepared than Sarah McCombie, a 22-year-old broker's assistant from Highams Park, London. Before leaving England Sarah had suffered a heavy bout of 'flu, which had confined her to her bed for the days preceding departure. Her parents counselled her against going, claiming she was in no fit state physically. Sarah, however, did not want to let anyone down. Her inclusion in the programme had come as a surprise to her. She only applied after she spotted someone in her office perusing the application form on the Web. She decided she would have a go, even though she had seen little of the first series. The occasional glimpse she caught showed the contestants lounging around the beaches under a blazing sun in a variety of bikinis. "I could do with some of that," she thought and as preparation she put in a couple of hours on a sunbed. "I didn't want to burn," she says. Nobody told her sunburn would be the least of her worries. As a luxury item she chose Vaseline – to soothe any painful burns and cuts, but more importantly to give her lips added gloss. "If I'm going to look like crap, then at least my lips'll look nice," was her reasoning. It went into her bag half an hour before she was due to leave for the airport, along with the rest of her stuff. It joined a minute pair of trainer socks and a thick, black woolly jumper, which got so wet on the canoe ride to South Island that it never dried out the whole time she was there. It was left behind – a gift to any fashion-conscious, or cold, island gods.

In stark contrast, Susannah Moffat's preparation was thorough and extensive. She read survival books, watched the video, and examined books about plants. She went orienteering on Dartmoor, visited the Living Rainforest Centre near Newbury and tried to identify plants and fruit and endlessly practised making knots and fire in the kitchen of her small terraced house in Wimbledon. She attempted to pile on weight, though failed when an illness over Christmas undid her "good work". She had sat down and thought deeply about her strategy and the way she would approach the show. "I've always had the dream of surviving and living off the land, pitting myself against nature. I have really enjoyed the outdoor life, walking, sports, camping, going off on bikes. I watched the first series and thought, 'That would be amazing. I could do things like that.' I was annoyed by so many of the contestants last time being so squeamish and pathetic and not using their initiative.

Jonny also prepared thoroughly – learning how to wring pheasants' necks in anticipation of getting the odd chicken or two as a reward. Others did not need such planning, like Alastair and John who had previous experience, or Bridget who worked on a farm. Others were less thorough, though some stout sacrifices had to be made: Dave Porter, an affable 55-year-old retired fireman from Newcastle, gave up brown ale for a week. He'd like to claim he put on weight for the challenge but the gut was his. When given a medical just before Christmas he inquired if he should shed a few pounds in weight. "No," was the doctor's reply, "it's best to go a few pounds overweight than under, because it best to lose fat rather than muscle." Dave broke out in a grin. "You'll do for me, kidda," he said, and proceeded to indulge himself merrily over the festive period.

Few were able to indulge themselves the night before the game, despite the advice offered by Ed Forsdick, who told them to get stuck into a hearty meal before they slept and an equally generous breakfast in the morning before they were collected. No one could eat – both Drew and Helen, who got a "nervous belly", spent more time on the toilet than in their respective beds, while the others tossed and turned restlessly – apart from Lee who had been like a coiled spring ever since leaving home and had exhausted himself by pacing the room all day. Meeta could not believe it was about to start, that she was to take part in such a huge production. Tayfun, meanwhile, was up all night preparing his smuggled items, sewing additional pairs of underpants into the lining of his allowed items of clothing and finding discreet places for his earplugs and sleeping tablets. He believed they would have four or five nights in Panama and had put off reading his survival books until the last minute. He had six hours in which to digest them all and hide his swag. He slept for an hour.

The next morning they were each woken by a representative of Planet 24 and taken to Albrook airport on the outskirts of Panama City. There they would board a chartered flight to Bocas del Toro where they would embark on the challenge of a lifetime.

Bocas del Toro is an archipelago of 68 islands on the Caribbean side of Panama. It lies just south of the Costa Rican border, between mainland Panama and the Caribbean Sea. The town of Bocas del Toro, nerve centre of the region despite its modest population of about 1,200, is on Isla Colon, the largest of the islands, which lies about 25 miles south of Costa Rica. Next to Colon lies Isla Bastimentos, part residential, but mostly national park. It has become a destination for young backpackers eager to snorkel and surf or simply idle away the hours in the sleepy town. Along with Spanish and English, visitors hear a unique local pidgin; a little Spanish, a little English, a little of the Guaymi Indian language that predates Columbus, all spoken with a Caribbean lilt.

The area has a rich history – Christopher Columbus "discovered" it in 1502; Sir Francis Drake plundered in these parts, as did a number of more bloodthirsty brigands, such as Henry Morgan, a feared pirate, who ruled the seas in the latter part of the seventeenth century. A cut-throat mercenary, he was prepared to go to any lengths to acquire wealth and notoriety. The ideal setting for *Survivor*, then. Rumour has it that on one of the islands Morgan buried his ill-gotten gains of gold and silver. Locals tell how for centuries those seeking the treasure have dug up almost every part of the island, without success. It was on that very same island that the North Island tribe were to be placed. But for the duration of their stay they were more interested in finding food than treasure.

Since December, members of the *Survivor* crew had been working on designing and building sets for the game. The logistics of the operation were far more complex than the first series when everything was set on the same island; camps, challenges, even the crew compound. Instead, in Bocas the crew lived in the main town – a sleepy place with the odd bar and restaurant, most of whose takings tripled over the seven weeks of filming and rehearsals – and had to take 15-mile boat rides to film on South and North Islands, and to Tribal Council, which was based on El Limbo. While the water through the mangrove swamps was often still, once the boats got out to sea the water became choppy, to say the very least. When the weather was at its worst, the condition of the sea deteriorated further. Green faces among crew and contestants were to become a common sight. On the island, the rules for the crew were simple: they must not speak to the survivors at any time unless to give directions or explain challenges; no watches could be worn in front of the survivors and eating, drinking or smoking in front of the contestants was forbidden. In addition to an English crew of 85, there were 25 local and 25 Argentinean crew, who had worked on other countries' versions of *Survivor* shot in South America. The presence of the Argentinean crew provided for some interesting clashes on the football pitch next to Bocas airport, when work afforded it. In a story now familiar to all English football fans, the Argentineans won the deciding encounter after each side had won one game apiece.

At Planet 24 in London, prior to filming the show, a team

had been developing the challenges and rule changes for the second series since July 2001. It was decided to trim the number of contestants from 16 to a more wieldy 12; an interactive element was to be incorporated to encourage viewer participation; new features such as Treemail were added and a few minor tweaks were made here and there. Most importantly, the challenges were made far harder than the first series – a true test of stamina, strength, endurance and mental agility. Coupled with the extreme weather conditions, it made the first series look like a teddy bears' picnic by comparison. This time, aside from the reward challenges, no extra food was given to the survivors other than three bananas each, which were provided at times when energy was needed but they were not able to hunt for their own food: one on the boat, one before they trekked into the jungle for two hours on the day they merged and one before the start of the Orientation Island challenge. They were accepted with relish. The rest of the time the contestants had to fend for themselves.

The twelve contestants – and reserves – were selected by a series of interviews across the country from 7,500 application forms received by Planet 24. A reasonable spread of personality types, ages and professions were sought; fierce arguments were held over who should and who should not be included, to ensure that the chosen dozen were representative of the British public. Favourites were fought for and discarded. Eventually, by mid-December, the selectors arrived at their final choices – give or take the odd withdrawal.

The location, while both dramatic and stunningly beautiful – when the sun shone at least – was host to innumerable dangers: in the island's tropical forest, over 300 species of plants have been recorded and 28 species of reptiles and amphibians including snakes and poisonous frogs. The most dangerous snake was the fer-de-lance viper, whose venom can kill within three or four hours; second deadliest is the Bushmaster, though that is rarely sighted; third in the biting order is the Coral Snake, but it is a timid creature more likely to run away than attack. Although the frogs were poisonous, a human being would have to ingest one to die of it. No one got so desperate that they took to cooking frogs, however. Other dangerous creatures included Orb and Fennel spiders, whose bite could potentially be fatal if not treated correctly.

The survivors would also share the islands with bats, monkeys, and scorpions as well as many other types of insects and bugs. Lurking around the mangroves were crocodiles, while sharks patrolled the waters. Portuguese Men o' War, the deadliest jellyfish on earth, were sighted beneath the surface of the sea. As well as the aforementioned coconuts, there were other natural hazards and diseases that could be contracted, some fatal. The most insidious is Leishmaniasis, caused by bacteria carried by a certain species of sand fly that proved a constant menace to the contestants. Usually, the bite manifests itself as a skin lesion or an ulcer but it can be more serious and can remain hidden for a year, with no outward sign of illness, until striking a person down. Mosquitoes are legion but the malaria risk on that side of Panama is low, though there is the risk of Dengue Fever, which may not be fatal but is hardly pleasant either. The contestants, however, were more likely to catch more mundane illnesses, like heat stroke, diarrhoea and infections from cuts. The other health risk came from accidents, of which there were far, far more than last year. While last year one crew member stood on a stingray and required treatment off Pulau Tiga, this year's list of wounded would have kept the scriptwriters of Casualty in plot lines for at least a series. Both cast and crew were accident prone, exacerbated by the extreme weather conditions and high seas. A trained medical team for contestants and crew was on at hand at all times, day and night.

Bocas del Toro has its own microclimate and the weather was unpredictable, to say the least. Whereas on Pulau Tiga the weather was humid yet pleasant, on Bocas it was wild and impossible to predict. At times it was biblical. The programme makers knew they would start filming at the close of the rainy season in Bocas. The wettest months are supposed to be December and July, with the dry season starting in late January and continuing through to the end of June. This was the tropics, however. For the first two weeks it was likely to rain but, rather than the expected occasional downpour, the rain was persistent and heavy. At night the weather was nowhere near as warm as people imagined, at least out at sea where the contestants were based, unsheltered from the elements by other land. Even the locals said they had never seen weather like it at that time of year. It would prove to be a true test of people's character and not everyone was up to that challenge.

Whatever the conditions, the survivors were filmed 24-hours-a-day, something that came as a shock to some members of the group, who clearly had not been listening when they were told this and were of the bizarre opinion that they would only be filmed for an hour or two a day. Helen, for example, walked in to the meeting room at the El Panama Hotel and, after seeing the lone camera in the corner, came to the conclusion that would be the extent of the filming through-out the whole event. She was given a shock, and was for once speechless, when she got off the plane at Bocas and was confronted by a phalanx of cameras. The constant filming was not welcomed by a number of the survivors – some of whom seemed to think that it would be a free holiday in paradise, a view that did not last long.

But on January 18, the final preparation for the start was under way. All that was required was for the contestants to be transported by plane, truck and boat towards their respective islands, in sight of which they would split into tribes and be cast adrift in the blue waters of the Caribbean. At Albrook they boarded the flight with the new presenter Mark Nicholas, a cameraman, a sound recordist and a director. If people weren't nervous before, they soon would be when Mark starting doing his piece to camera. As he told people, "This is *Survivor*!" Helen looked out of the window, desperately trying to stifle her giggles, while Dave thought, "Who's the clean-cut feller with the bouffant talking to?" Nobody could accuse this group of being TV-savvy, or of seeking fifteen minutes of fame.

After landing they disembarked and were led into the main, and only, hall at Bocas airport where they were ordered to sit down. To the side sat two more reserves who, they were told, would be substitutes should anyone be found trying to smuggle illicit items on to the island. All twelve were given one final chance to hand over any goods concealed upon them, with the warning that if anything was found during the body search then they would be disqualified. Hearing this, Tayfun got up and approached the desk behind which Mark stood, unaware he was about to witness an admission to the greatest act of smuggling since the Trojan Horse. Tayfun proceeded to pull out reams and reams of items – "It was like a magician pulling things from a hat," is Dave's recollection – to the astonishment of everyone. He had made the first big mistake and the game had not even officially started.

"I thought everybody would smuggle something, or at least try," he says now. "They all did it last time – Charlotte had stuff in her bra. I thought everyone would try to get a few things on. All the things I brought I thought would be of advantage to my tribe. They wouldn't complain if all of a sudden I produced fire. Everyone benefits. I didn't think smuggling would piss any of the other contestants off. I thought they would check and what they would find they would confiscate. So I had loads, intending most of it to be found. Everything I really wanted was in my jock strap in my pants. In there I had matches and a lighter and a penknife, sleeping tablets, ear plugs, extra vitamins, chewing gum from the States with fluoride. I thought it would last my tribe to the merger. I had things scattered everywhere. I even replaced my malaria tablets with vitamins."

Ed Forsdick was furious. He had made a point of telling everyone not to try and smuggle. Security was much tighter than for the first series to make living conditions that much tougher. What, after all, is the point of making people bust a gut to win fire if someone is allowed to waltz onto the island with a box of matches in their underpants? He took a sheepish-looking Tayfun outside the building and gave him what might be politely termed a "ticking off". "If you've got anything else then you'd better hand it in now," he demanded. Sure enough Tayfun tripped off to the gents, heaven knows what he rid himself of, and emerged looking even more sheepish. This was a difficult humiliation from which to recover, as he recognises.

"Firstly, I thought 'I have just made myself stand out in front of the others.' Secondly, the show's executive producer is going mad at me. This is not going to be a good experience. I had just handed my tribe mates an excuse to alienate me and I've cheesed off the people in charge of how I will be portrayed on television. I might just as well go home. I said to Ed, 'OK, obviously I've upset you. I didn't mean to. Right, I'm off.' I knew from that point I couldn't win. He took me by the arm and he said, 'No, you're staying. We've gone through a lot of work and effort to get you out here.' I went into the toilet and got rid of everything. They took it all. If I had known it would be that serious I would never have done it. I said to Ed, 'I'm not going to survive here. I've given them an easy excuse to vote me off. It also makes me look more competitive than the others. On those two fronts I am blown out of the water. I'm not going to last.' Ed said to me, 'They'll need you physically, so hang on and see what happens.' "

Tayfun and the others were then subjected to a rigorous search and it was discovered another survivor had some hidden contraband: Dave. In his back pocket was a comb. Unlike Tayfun, however, Dave's was a case of sheer absent-mindedness but he still got worried. "I was thinking, 'Oh no, I'm going to be disqualified, man. What a dickhead.' I said to them, 'Haway, it was a genuine mistake.' They believed me and it was all right. For a minute though, I thought I'd had it." With the search over, the contestants were weighed and then marched onto a truck and driven to the pier in Bocas and the awaiting boat that would take them out to their islands. Each was handed an envelope with their tribal colours, but they were prevented from opening them until the signal came, two minutes before they were ordered overboard. Still they had to remain silent.

Once on board Drew immediately got sick. She had not eaten breakfast, contrary to instructions. It was now mid-afternoon and the weather was scorching, and they had had little to eat. At one point she was on her hands and knees vomiting and there was concern among the medics and the crew about her condition. Should she be allowed to go ahead? After a quick examination by Dr Johnson it was agreed that it was nothing serious, probably heat stroke. It was still an unpleasant experience for Drew, the crowning point of a bewildering 24 hours.

"Everything hit me. I felt really anxious about everything. Part of that is me, I do get anxious when faced with new situations; another part was that everybody else had a long time to prepare for the show and being on it. I really didn't know until the night before and I think that had a lot to do with it. I was seasick, suffering from heat stroke and I felt awful. I had not been able to eat anything and I was throwing up on the boat and it felt like, 'If I feel this bad on the first day then there is no way I will last this out.' Another part of me felt disheartened because I wasn't going to last a second on the island. I was going to be useless. I wanted it, but I felt like physically it wasn't going to be for me. It occurred to me that perhaps I wasn't as physically tough as I thought. On the boat I went downstairs and told Ed that I felt ill; I had the worst stomach cramps I had ever had in my life. I was in so much pain. I said to Ed: 'I feel so ill that I really don't believe I'm going to be able to jump off the boat and swim because I'm in so much pain.' Then the doctor saw me and said it was my choice but that I would probably feel much better when I got in the water. It would cool me down. He persuaded me and I did jump in and I have to be honest: when I hit the water I felt 100 per cent better. On the canoe I threw up and I threw up all the way but by the time we reached the island I felt fine. From that moment I didn't look back. I never felt as ill as that again."

Drew wasn't in the mood for talking, so she didn't join in the chat when the survivors were allowed to speak to each other for the first time. Everyone went around greeting everybody else "like a bloody dinner party", remembers Lee. Alastair made an impression on Jonny immediately when he was asked what he did. "I'm a fuel cards salesman" was his response and he went in to immense detail about the job. As Jonny points out, people don't tend to supply a job description when they've merely been asked what they do for a living. They wait until they are asked. Immediately he marked Alastair down as one to watch. The others swallowed his fib though and it must be said in his defence that he might have made things difficult for himself had he answered correctly. "I'm a managing director of an oil distribution firm that has a turnover of more than £80m a year and my salary is well in excess of £100,000 per annum. Oh, and I live in a castle," might have got people's backs up. The conversation continued, everyone trying to make the best impression they could, apart from Bridget, who answered Tayfun's initial inquiry in typically blunt fashion.

"What did you think of what happened back at the airport," he asked tentatively. "I think you were a complete prat," she replied without hesitation.

It was to get worse.

A Hard Rain is Gonna Fall

Your average machete blade is made of steel, a combination of iron ore and carbon. How dense is iron ore? Dense enough for it to sink when thrown in to water. How dense is a Cambridge mathematics graduate who thinks it will float? Extremely. Perhaps Tayfun was too busy dancing when he should have been attending lectures and learning about his metals. Whatever, the one job he was given when the tribes were given two minutes to salvage everything they could from the boat before jumping overboard, he blew. It was his second big mistake of the day. His explanation was that he was afraid that if he plunged into the water with the machete in his hand he might injure himself. Before leaving England, he had watched videos of the first two American series of *Survivor* to help plan his strategy. In the second series, one of the contestants had fallen in the fire at Tribal Council and been burnt and scarred for life. This was a fate Tayfun wished to avoid.

"The night before Stephen Flett [the programme's psychologist] had come to my room and asked me a question. 'What is the very worst thing that could happen to you in this game?' Some people, I guess, said being kicked off first, or to get to the last two and not win. None of that mattered to me – it could happen, and I would have to accept it. I thought about it and I knew the one thing that would have ruined it for me was to come out with a severe injury.

"So there I am on the boat. I was looking at this machete and I had just slashed the rope. I put it in its sheath and thought that if it came out then it could do some serious damage. I thought maybe this was fate. I thought there might have been a reason for that conversation the night before. I paused and thought about it. It feels light and I thought the sheath might keep it afloat. I decided I did not want to jump into the sea with this in my hand. If it was to come out in the water and hit my face, or my eye, then God knows. I threw it in thinking I could jump in and grab it. Well, I threw it in and it just sank."

Survivor is not for the timid. Realising how stupid he had been, it went through his mind to pretend that it had got lost or come up with some other explanation. But remembering how Nick, the hapless, hopeless first survivor voted off Pulau Tiga in the first series, had come a cropper trying to cover up his machete mistake, Tayfun decided to confess immediately, as Dave recollects. "We were all on board bar one when this little head pops up at the side of the canoe and goes, 'Sorry guys, I lost the machete'. I could have hit him over the head with an oar, I swear. My first thought was, 'Well get down there and get it' I said, 'You've done whaaaaat?' And he says, 'I thought it would float.' And I thought, 'Who the hell's this kid?' Then I said, 'Haway son, get on board.' But what a bloody idiot." It did not improve Dave's mood, which had been dented when the contestants had opened their envelopes and been given their tribal colours. He was in North Island and their colour was red. Dave is a rabid, fanatical Newcastle United supporter; their arch-rivals are neighbouring Sunderland, "Mackems", as Newcastle fans know them derogatorily. They play in red.

"I couldn't believe it when we opened the envelopes and the t-shirts were red – the bloody Mackems! I thought, 'Oh no! Me mates at home will slaughter us.' I never ever wear red; there's nothing in the house that's red, nothing. I won't have anything to do with it. It's war between us and Sunderland, y'know. I had a go at Ed. I said, 'What are you trying to do to us man!' Anyway, I had to put it on."

Dave's mood was buoyed by the sight of Alastair, whose strength would obviously be of great value. Tayfun finally clambered on board and they got under way. But Tayfun's foolishness had handed Dave and Alastair the perfect reason to bond and all the way to the island they made jibes about the machete, telling him not to worry about it but then adding, "But who thinks that metal floats?" It was going to be a long way back from here for Tayfun. He had said his strategy was to appear slightly incompetent and play up to the stereotypical image of a dancer being a bit of a bimbo. Though it wouldn't do him any good whatsoever, he had certainly succeeded.

Academically, Tayfun is anything other than a bimbo, having a first in Maths from Cambridge. It was at Cambridge that he started dancing again after a football injury in his teens had left him certain he would never be able to attempt anything athletic again. But after only a few years of dancing for Cambridge, he became involved in the pre-amateur circuit and then was plucked from obscurity by Vibeke Toft – the "Viking" who also plucks his eyebrows – who is one of the best female Latin-American dancers in the world and who selected Tayfun to be her partner. Tayfun bypassed amateur level and is now among the world's best. In fact, he was due to move to Los Angeles when he was selected for *Survivor*, a show he had first seen in the US and then followed avidly in Britain. The move was postponed until after filming finished. In preparation, he had been a keen student of tactics and thought intensely about the game.

"I made sure I was trained up, and did loads of running and swimming. I tried to put on weight by eating crap. I had loads of Caramel Frappucinos. Then I watched the US videos, watched the UK video, and read the book. It would have helped me had my tribe learned more about the first series of *Survivor*. They were full of things like, 'We shouldn't form alliances until we make the merger.' They tried to play it nice, nice, nice the whole way through, without realising that only two can make the final and if you're part of a group where some are closer than the others, you must figure out where you rank – if you're not in the first three, then you're in the wrong alliance."

The mood on North's canoe improved considerably – apart from Drew who was too busy vomiting over the side – when they looked behind them and saw that South were sinking. They had been successful at least in getting all the equipment and all their personnel overboard, and even tied their belongings to the back of the canoe so as not to overload it, unlike North who had simply slung everything on the boat. But it did them no good. As soon as all six took their seats, the boat started taking in water. According to John, "We got in and it was 'glug, glug, glug'. The boxes were behind us, not even in it. The seats weren't connected to the boat – they just slid into place – and they started floating off. It was really embarrassing. I felt really incompetent. Meanwhile, they were gliding like swans across the water."

This was the beginning of what would become a bugbear for South: the belief that their canoe was defective. Ed Forsdick dismisses the claim; he says that all canoes are different and it was pure incompetence on South's behalf. Every single member of the team is adamant, however, that they had been dealt a bad hand, with John, as ever, the most vocal in complaining. "I remember being on the boat before we were told to jump overboard and looking at the canoes being towed behind us. One was really narrow and I remember thinking, 'I hope I'm not in the blue team because their canoe looks really crap'. And sure enough I was in the blue team and it was crap. Ed said it could still be propelled forwards even if it was taking in water. But it sank in about five seconds and was seriously unstable. We'd have been better off with a tin bath, I tell you."

With a distance to travel to each island, and the fact that they had not hit the water until after 5pm, it was no surprise that both tribes arrived at their respective islands after dark. Soaking wet, hungry and tired, they realised the first harsh fact about their environment: the weather could be cold. Wet clothing did not help, but it was a salutary reminder to those who were expecting paradise that conditions were not going to be easy at all. This was bolstered further when it became clear that building a shelter in pitch darkness was not going to be possible. They would just have to sleep out in the open. Then it started to rain. Sarah McCombie started to sing but was promptly told to shut up. Still, she chatted away telling stories. One had her tribe mates in hysterics. It came after the tribe had been discussing how, in the past, lonely, sex-starved sailors used to, ahem, seek pleasure in the company of a skate. This segued into a tale about a friend of hers who worked for what we will politely call a leading food emporium. The rest is in Sarah's words: "He used to work where the gammon is, right. He used to get the gammon, make a hole in it and then have sex with it. Then he would just seal it up when he finished. I asked him how many times he did it and he said about 70!" Sarah, Jonny and Lee were all in stitches. Out to one side lay Bridget, worrying that she might have to throttle Sarah because she was like her two daughters, "twittering on and on about crap". Also off to one side was John, who was feeling very low.

John entered *Survivor* knowing that he had a good chance. He knew the game well having seen the American show while he was living in Australia. In fact he and his friends used to hold a tribal council to vote people out of their house. Coming from a sporting background – his father, who died when John was a boy, was an Olympic weightlifter – he knew he was fit and strong. He was in the Marines for five years until the age of 22 so he knew basic survival skills and had no doubts about his mental strength, having served in the Gulf War and in Northern Ireland. The latter was a tough experience for more reasons than the obvious; it is his homeland. On patrol on the streets he was a "Brit bastard"; while back at barracks he was a "Paddy bastard". He witnessed friends being killed, and the stress of seeing members of his family while he was guarding army checkpoints. He was happy to leave, having, he says, seen "the writing on the wall". Other people he knew left the Marines and were forced to take jobs as security guards and the like. He wanted something more challenging, so he retrained and began a career in physiotherapy, which he enjoyed but he needed a more cerebral challenge. He retrained once more and became a barrister.

He knew he would be able to cope with the challenges and, given his competitive nature, that was what he was looking forward to the most. His only worry was that he had become too soft since leaving the Marines. He admits that he asks his girlfriend to go out and bring the car to the front door when it's raining so he doesn't get too wet. Even though in the Marines a fair amount of time was spent outdoors, it was something he was forced to do and he has rarely camped since. "I have never been particularly hard or robust," he says. "I'm not some ex-army nutcase who goes away for the weekend, living in the wild." As he lay in the dark listening to the others pass the time with idle chit-chat, he began to doubt himself.

"That first night, I thought 'I'm going to be the first person voted off.' I thought I had nothing in common with the others. Two of them were from the Essex area and they were being really chirpy about it. It just transported me back 15 years to my first night in the Marines. I thought, 'This is just hideous. I remember why I left'. It was freezing, pitch black and I thought, 'You haven't thought this through. This is not going to be pleasant.' I watched the last series and thought it would be glitzy, beaches, sarongs, captions flashing up on screen saying, 'Sekutu Beach – 98 degrees'. Everyone seemed to spend their time sunbathing, breaking off to think who they were going to vote off next. After literally ten minutes it was obvious they were going to make it harder this time. The first night everyone was trying to cheer each other up; Jonny was being really funny with Susannah, so they got on well really quickly; Lee and Sarah were peas in a pod; Bridget was quite quiet but I just did not feel the inclination to talk to anyone at all. I lay there the first night thinking I would be there for only three days then I'd be voted off. I didn't get an opinion of them until the next day and then I realised they were not as good as I thought they were, as fit or strong. They were just regular, incompetent people."

After much stubbing of feet and tripping over, North Island had also decided to sleep in the open. The next morning they awoke and, according to Dave, "everyone just clicked", though we can presume he meant everyone but Tayfun. It is unlikely that Dave had ever come into contact with any Latin American male dancers who shave their legs and pluck their eyebrows. To Dave, *paso doble* is a Spanish fullback. They slept on the beach, with Tayfun being teased incessantly about his machete mistake. Just as they were drifting off to sleep, however, the rain came again. Bewildered, they all got up and lay down behind their tribal flag, which would have been fine had the rain fallen horizontally and not vertically. They got just as wet. A shelter was a necessity.

At first light, work began on building a shelter, with Alastair at the forefront. He had already taken a look at his tribe and pronounced himself "a wee bit disappointed". He sensed – correctly as it turned out – that South had a stronger team, physically, though he admits to completely underestimating Drew. He wasn't to be the only one.

"What we had was an 'old and bold' man in Dave, like a father figure in some respect, but not a grandfather figure as someone commented; Helen, who almost immediately seemed mature beyond her years. She's a brilliant girl. She was very enthusiastic and I didn't know she had experience in this sort of thing. There was Drew who had obviously prepared a bit, knew what she was doing but was quite quiet and withdrawn initially, almost to the point where you think, 'Hmm, what's this girl all about, can't really suss her out,' whereas with Dave, Helen and Meeta you knew straight away what they were about. Tay seemed a bit dodgy and Meeta I was also unsure about."

Helen's previous experience to which Alastair refers is a trip she undertook for Operation Raleigh to Belize, where she worked for four months. She has also worked as a holiday rep and for the Camp America programme as well as completing a degree at Sheffield Hallam University. For a 22-year-old woman she had certainly packed a lot into her short life. Despite her travels she is also extremely close to her family in Sheffield, and a lot of family there is too – 57 cousins to be exact, who mostly live in the surrounding area. Her grandparents live next door to her family home, while an auntie lives in a neighbour-ing street. Living among others and having to share is second nature, given that her house often resembles Grand Central Station. She was extremely surprised to be selected for *Survivor*, though not half as shocked as her mother who works as a cleaner at Sheffield Town Hall. When Helen was told that she had made the programme, she called her mother who let forth an ear-splitting scream that had the councillors of Sheffield scurrying for cover. Helen is a mix of the naive and the worldly and Alastair was impressed. In the sea with Dave that day he admitted that he was strongly attracted to her.

They managed to construct their shelter – or rather Alastair and Dave did, while Tayfun was still being punished for his error of the previous day, which forced North to use a spade to cut ropes, with the threat that posed for people's digits. While Dave and Alastair performed the strong-arm tasks, Tayfun was reduced to helping the women dress the shelter with palm fronds. His fastidiousness manifested itself on several occasions that day, in particular when he constantly went to the water to wash his hands whenever they got sandy or sticky. His position within the tribe was built on shifting sand; less than 24 hours on the island and three members said in interviews that they would be voting him off should the chance arise. Realising he was vulnerable, Tayfun decided to keep his mouth shut and earn back the respect of his tribe mates. He was not as anonymous as Drew, who retreated so far into the background that it would have been no surprise had she sprouted leaves and a few coconuts. To be fair to Drew, however, she is not naturally gregarious, particularly among strangers, and she was still getting used to the dramatic change in her circumstances.

On South Island they discovered they had a natural food source in the shape of coconuts. Not being able to make fire, this was the only nourishment they would get. They all ate, even though Sarah was not too enamoured by the food. She was even less pleased when she saw Bridget being sick. She reasoned that this was because of the coconut, rather than mild heat stroke and a migraine, the probable cause. From that point Sarah did not eat another thing until she left the island. Already she was emerging as a favourite to be voted off, despite her entertainment value and her friendship with Lee. As the others built the shelter, she stood back and watched, arms folded. The only moment she came alive was when she had the chance to put on her bikini and go for a swim. She knew she was out of place from that point on.

"They thought I was funny and just laughed at me. I didn't have a clue. Bridget asked if I had done anything like this before and I said, 'I don't tend to sit in the garden and build fire.' They were running about everywhere, picking things up and carrying them about. They never stopped. I did not know what to do, didn't have a clue. I knew they were doing things wrong, though. They tried for 24 hours to make fire and I knew they couldn't do it. It was pissing with rain, everything was wet but they kept trying. I knew it wasn't going to happen. I just went and rinsed my bikini out or something. Everyone else was like, 'Let's build a shelter,' or, 'Let's get some more bamboo sticks' and they were so into it. I was like, 'Can't we just go swimming?' I have never ever been camping – I'm used to five-star hotels and beer and loads of food. I don't know why but I assumed there would be loads of fruit and I thought, 'Blinding'. I could eat fruit every day. I mean, I would rather have a kebab or something but I could deal with it. It was a bog pit. We couldn't even swim because the currents were too strong. It was an ugly island. The weather was rubbish."

In contrast, Jonny, who the previous morning in the hotel had woken at 5am to tie the table in his room to his bed to help perfect his knots, seemed at ease in the surroundings, while Susannah used her preparation to wander the island identifying bread fruit, limes and lime leaves. Within five minutes, according to John, she had managed to identify every part of the island's flora and fruit. He was impressed. "It was brilliant. I was thinking, 'She's a God. Lift her up in a big chair and let's make a sacrifice to her.' " For his part, John supervised the shelter construction as subtly as he could without giving away his Marine background. All three were getting on well. Lee was mucking in admirably but there was a sense that he was more at home having a laugh with Sarah. Bridget, her illness aside, was utterly at home with the outdoor life and was not fazed by anything, other than her close proximity to people rather than sheep.

She had no qualms about eating whatever was available or "killing animals and stuff like that". She knew she could build shelters and make fire, something she would turn into a cottage industry during her stay. Like John, she had no time for idle chitchat but she was satisfied with her tribe. "They seemed a sensible bunch. We all had different talents and different backgrounds and as the day progressed we all started to get on. To begin with we all got hungry. I got a migraine and started throwing up right, left and centre. I got my medicine, took it and had a couple of days of throbbing headaches but since then I didn't suffer a single headache. But someone said it was like a detoxifying diet. All we were having was coconut and water and that was it for four days. People spend £500 or more for that sort of treatment in London."

The most important occurrence of that second day, in either tribe, was the alliance struck between John and Jonny. Both realised they got on well and shared a sense of humour. At a quiet moment together, the deal was struck. The way John tells it, while trying, and failing abysmally, to get a fire going, Jonny turned to him and said, "I know it's early to start thinking of alliances but if you're thinking of somebody can you consider me?" John was flattered, having made a mental note not to approach anyone until they had approached him. "Plus I didn't know how to start making an alliance. It's like chatting girls up when you're 14. What do you do? What do you say? 'Er, excuse me but will you form an alliance with me?' No, Jonny saved me making a right prat out of myself," he remembers. It was something Jonny had planned from the start and he hoped to reinforce the alliance by recruiting Susannah over the coming day: it was believed she was the most competent of the women, and would be able to find out what was going on among the others.

Susannah and Lee were getting on well but there was a clash of cultures. The young professionals, John, Jonny, and Susannah – or the Hampstead Dinner Party as one crew member dubbed them – all migrated towards each other and away from Lee and Sarah. Bridget was simply Bridget and did her own thing. Ironically, the reverse was true on North where Tayfun, who would feel at home at a Hampstead dinner party, was made to feel an outcast, a freak even, by his tribe mates, who revelled in each other's regional accents. Class was definitely to become a factor and would continue to be – so would snobbery, and as the game progressed, reverse snobbery.

The next day saw the first Immunity Challenge – there was no reward in the first cycle, it being agreed that the contestants needed a day to settle in and construct their camps. They were picked up and taken to Isla Bastimentos where a punishing assault course had been constructed that would test everyone to the limit, especially considering they were all desperately lacking food and several had been ill and felt weak. On seeing the course South realised that Sarah, who does not exercise ("I tried running once but I hated it") would be a liability. This was confirmed when they walked the course beforehand and she was exhausted by that effort. She was not alone in that respect – Meeta was also struggling after merely strolling around and began to have doubts about what she had let herself in for.

Sarah decided to confess her chronic lack of fitness to her

tribe, not that they needed to be told. They had guessed. "I told them I couldn't do it," she remembers. "Lee said I would be all right. I thought I was going to pass out just walking round. I said they would have to carry me because we hadn't eaten in four days and the sun was really strong that day. It had been freezing cold and then there was this bright sunshine. If I hadn't been ill I think I would have done better. They told me to go off in front and sprint and if I was in bits then they would drag me through it. The first bit I ran but then all I remember – I don't remember much – was going 'Oh my God'. I thought I was going to die. I couldn't breathe. At one point I couldn't talk. I was looking for the medical men. They had to drag me around until I got my breath back. I thought my chest was going to cave in."

South got their tactics right while North were a complete mess, with stragglers here, there and everywhere. There was a confrontation at the cargo net when Dave's ample figure prevented anyone getting through alongside him. He lifted the net when he reached the other end, helping Lee and Sarah. "Thanks mate. Thanks a bunch," Lee said genuinely. Dave, however, thought he was being sarcastic and immediately took a dislike to Lee. "Typically bloody cockney," is his view, "Thinks he's done it all and knows it all." Dave, like Bridget is no fan of London. "I hate that bloody place. I cannot stand it. Everybody's miserable; nobody talks to you and the people that do talk to you are all foreign anyway." Learning that Tayfun lived in London did little to improve Dave's opinion of him.

The critical moment in the challenge occurred after the beam, with which Susannah struggled terribly. Her balance, she concedes, is not one of her strongest points and, after she fell off it once, her confidence deserted her and from that point on she kept falling off. She panicked when she noticed that Helen and Meeta, who had been dawdling at the back of the field, were beginning to catch her up. So when she finally crossed the beam she made a beeline for the rest of her team, ignoring a hurdle she needed to climb over. Meeta nearly made an identical mistake but was spotted by Tayfun who bellowed at her to go over the hurdle. It probably saved him. If he had not done that then North would also have been disqualified, South would have won and, given Alastair and Dave's antipathy towards him and Alastair's increasing dominance over his tribe, Tayfun would have gone for certain. His quick-wittedness earned little thanks from his tribe, however.

South recovered from Susannah's troubles on the beam to go on and finish first convincingly and celebrated in jubilant fashion. Unfortunately, twenty minutes later, they were distraught when Mark announced that Susannah's error had got her team disqualified. It was North's turn to celebrate. Tayfun attempted to sympathise with Susannah, telling her not to worry and that he had lost the machete. At that point, two decisions were made: first, South decided never to celebrate a victory again until Mark announced who had won. The paranoia over disqualification caused both tribes to badger Ed Forsdick before each challenge with the question, "What do we have to do to get disqualified?" After a time the question started to drive him mad. Susannah could not believe what she had done. She had put so much in effort into preparing for *Survivor* and she thought she had just undone all that work with one stupid error.

The second, and more important, decision made at that point was made by Sarah: she wanted to go. She explains why.

"They were so gutted by losing and I wasn't that bothered. Susannah was in bits and I didn't want her to get voted off because she messed up. They wanted it so badly and I just wasn't that bothered, so it was only fair that I went. I may have been voted off anyway but if I hadn't then I would have been stuck there, not wanting to stay, while someone who really wanted it, and had worked hard, would have to go. They asked me to think about it but my mind was made up. If we had won the challenge then I would have made the most of it and it may have got better, I may have enjoyed it more. But I was worried about getting stuck there. After that challenge, for the 15 minutes or so when we thought we'd won, I was pleased and happy to be there. I wanted to stick it out and I really liked my tribe. That was the reason I did what I did. We got on so well and they loved it there. I couldn't wait to have a beer. When I was voted off it was like a weight lifted off my shoulders."

South had to stand and watch North take the immunity idol and, even more galling, waterproof matches that would enable them to cook that evening and have rice with the eggs they had also won. South would go hungry yet again. That night Susannah confessed to camera that she was between two alliances; Lee on the one hand, and Jonny and John on the other. "I am going to have to let one of them down and that one of them is Lee, because Jonny and John are far stronger," she said. There was also the fact that she saw the three of them to be "professionals on a certain level". Immediately after confessing this, Lee sauntered over and Susannah, her background in drama paying dividends, managed to deflect his enquiries over whether they were to stay firm. "I want to remain flexible," she added. Lee says he felt sorry for Susannah after the challenge and that he thought she needed a friend. It was obvious to him that the two Johns were tight and he needed to form a counter-alliance and Susannah was ideal. He felt, given how vulnerable she was feeling, she would bite his arm off if he offered a help-ing hand. He was wrong: she stabbed him in the back instead.

Sarah then announced to the tribe that she wanted out. "I so, so need a kebab," she shouted. "I want a hotel room and I want a bed and I want a shower and I want some dinner and I won't be going camping ever again." Not that she had ever been camping in the first place. The others responded by asking if she was sure and accepted her request. John told the camera that she would have gone anyway and then spoke about how he had no time for facile conversations: this from a man, bear in mind, who later spent 24 hours on a log talking nonsense, asking people what their top five soft rock ballads were and if they liked Captain Pugwash. That night the topic for debate in the shelter was Sarah's future after the show. For £50,000 she said she would have no hesitation in "getting her bangers out" for the newspapers. All this talk was proving too much for Lee, who admitted he was in danger of getting a "peck on". "The first male arousal in three days," trumpeted Jonny. John meanwhile kept out of this facile conversation and drifted off to sleep humming "The Final Countdown" by Europe. By the same time the next day they would be five, and probably stronger for it.

Sarah's confession helped to lighten South's mood by relieving them from having to conspire about who they would have to vote off. As Sarah spent the day trying to work out whether to leave or pack her sodden black jumper, the rest of her tribe analysed their opponents and came to the conclusion that North were less organised then they were. Alastair, Jonny was now certain, was trying to deceive everyone and had emerged as leader; Dave seemed genial and inoffensive; Tayfun a bit odd; Meeta and Helen were lightweights while Drew, well, she was "miserable", "unsmiling" and "dreary". It was not until they met and got to know her that she would shake the "Dreary Drew" tag among South Island. For her part, Drew admits it takes a long time to get to know her and that it takes her time to adjust to new situations. She was someone who would get stronger the longer she survived.

Buoyed by their victory, North were also examining their

rivals. They had marked John out as leader and developed a healthy respect for Jonny; Lee was mistrusted because of the misunderstanding over his comments to Dave at the challenge, Susannah they knew little of and the same with Bridget. They found Sarah funny and expected her to be the person ejected from the island, helped on her way by a few catty comments from Meeta about Essex girls and white stilettos. They were relaxed, most of them having taken the decision not to worry about alliances before the merger. Even Tayfun was feeling more secure, having been instrumental in preventing his tribe being disqualified. Dave and Alastair were still going on about the machete, however, even though they had won an axe at the immunity challenge, and it was clear that his position was still a perilous one.

"I was isolated. They would shunt me off to do something else. The guys blocked me out. Carrying the water, they wouldn't let me carry it saying, 'It's just the two of us' as if to reinforce their bond and my exclusion. They did that in front of the girls as if they were sending them a message. Alastair would say patronising things to them like, 'I don't want to lose any of our girls'. When they lost Sarah, he was saying, 'I wouldn't like to lose any of ours.' So he was hanging out with Dave all the time and he did not want to lose the girls. So whom does that leave? His brainwashing was unsubtle, and his exclusion of me was blatant."

Meeta was not happy either; despite being critical of Sarah, she was suffering a similar problem, the realisation that she had got involved with something for which she was ill suited and ill prepared. It had come as a shock to her because she felt that, given her life experiences, she could cope with any hardship. She was orphaned in her mid-teens while at an Indian boarding school and was raised by her brother, Amit, who is two years older than her. She has had to scrap for everything she has achieved in her life. Everything she has ever striven for she has attained and she believed that *Survivor* would be no different. She had done intensive work at the gym and as a special constable for six years she was used to coping with difficult challenges. Like John, she had watched the previous year's show and been seduced by the look of it; glistening waters, snorkelling in the shallows, all that she could cope with. Instead, that first night she had sat rocking herself, and had done so since, simply for comfort. Stephen Flett asked when she came off if her mother had rocked her to sleep as a child and it emerged that she had. Beneath her brash, upbeat and colourful exterior she was deeply unhappy on the island. The sheer physical effort of that first challenge added to the burgeoning feeling that she was unsuited to what lay ahead.

"The assault course killed me and from then on I wasn't happy. I got through because of Alastair and Helen; she waited for me every step of the way and somehow they dragged me through it. I thought I was going to lose my breath – at the beginning, at the top of the hill. We had not eaten, you see. Eventually, I fell down the hill and nearly landed on a camera-man's head. I cut my legs really badly, sliced off the top of my big toe and hurt my knee. I had no energy whatsoever. I saw Susannah miss the hurdle and told my tribe and they thought I was so weak that I was seeing things. They didn't believe me. I nearly didn't go over the hurdle. Tayfun shouted and told me. I did it because of him. I cried when they lost, not because I was glad we had won but because I had thought I had let them down. I was disappointed because I wanted to go home. The next day I told them I wanted to go if we went to Tribal Council.

"To be honest, I entered *Survivor* to see what it was like; to enter the challenges and live on the island. I have done things in my career like that. I went to the gym but obviously didn't do the right stuff. I didn't imagine it would be anything like that. I knew it would be physically challenging, but this time it was hardcore. I was not alone; a few of us thought there would be coral reefs, sunbathing. Jesus Christ, were we wrong."

Day four also saw the weather worsen, the rain becoming increasingly persistent and prolonged and it remained wild for the next fortnight. The currents in the sea became stronger and fishing was too dangerous a pastime. Taking the boat out to fish could easily result in someone being swept away. A valuable source of protein was ruled out so the survivors contented themselves with hunting on land for tiny crabs, which provided a meagre meal. North had no Susannah – someone who could identify edible fruit and plants. But on the other hand, they did have fire. Aside from falling coconuts, frogs, snakes and dangerous currents, Meeta had discovered another danger – except in this case it was pride that was imperilled. "One morning I was answering a call of nature and a helicopter flew past, with a camera pointed right at me. It was a bit much for me. I said to Al, 'They've got my arse on camera.' He said, 'Don't worry, Meeta. It won't fit on the screen.' "

The first visit to the new, minimalist yet visually stunning Tribal Council was South's pleasure. The rain was pouring down and there was little protection for the contestants. It just served to persuade Sarah that she had been right in asking to go. There were few regrets as the votes were revealed, though there were a few surprises when it emerged that Sarah's vote had been against John. This was on Lee's insistence and was all part of his plan to break the John and Jonny alliance at some point in the future. It backfired somewhat, though, revealing to the others that Lee was perfectly capable of playing the game. It singled him out, made him look like a player and

John took a mental note to watch out for him.

Sarah hugged everyone before leaving and then went off for that long-awaited beer. She was delayed by having to record an interview with Mark once her former tribe mates had gone and then further delayed when her boat broke down on the way to the Buccaneer, where evicted contestants would spend the night when they were voted off. Given how rough the water was, it wasn't a pleasant experience and ensured that the first bottle of local beer "Soberana" never touched the sides. Next day she underwent a debriefing by Stephen Flett and was flown to Panama City where she spent a night before flying home to the creature comforts she had missed so much. Leaving so soon did present a few problems, however, considering she had informed friends that she had taken a job in Argentina for a couple of months as a cover story to explain her absence. When she arrived back after a week she was lucky enough to blame her swift return on the febrile state of the Argentinean economy and the insurgence that stemmed from that. All her tribe mates remembered her fondly. Only John lost his temper with her, and that was on the final day when she knew she was going home.

"The effort of getting the canoe out to sea when it had beached was tremendous. Just trying to overcome the inertia took everyone's strength. There we were around it, trying to drag it in and it was not budging. I turned around and Sarah was just lying in the boat, knackered. I swore and told her to get out. That was the only time I lost it with her. But she was hilarious; some of her stories and her clothes were just unbelievable. She's the sort of girl you can imagine being a scream down the pub but she wasn't really suited for the conditions we met. In fact, I've never met anyone less prepared."

There was one positive consequence of Tribal Council: fire. South Island were able to take their lit torches back with them, which meant that for the first time in four days South could cook rice. With the lime leaves Susannah had found they could also flavour the rice. But when they got back to camp the rain was so heavy lighting the fire was impossible. They had to wait for the next morning for their first meal. But this advancement for the tribe served also to set Lee back. They found a spoon that washed up on the beach and after washing it in the sea and then burning it to kill any bacteria they decided to use it as a communal spoon, eating a mouthful and then passing it around. Lee, worried about hygiene, spurned the spoon, choosing to eat with his fingers. This gave the others the impression that he was picky and it was another black mark against his name. Susannah was explaining her thinking to camera. Jonny and John were strong, capable of winning challenges, and knew their Chardonnay from their Chateauneuf du Pape. Lee, meanwhile, was more a lager top lad, and he had a temper. He was looking vulnerable. South Island needed to win.

'They done me like a kipper'

The next challenge, the first Reward Challenge, turned out to be a complete and unmitigated disaster for South Island. First, it involved getting in their hated canoe, which was bad enough; second, and more detrimentally for their hopes of winning, it also required a modicum of skill and coordination. They had tried to psych themselves up beforehand, though reading the Treemail indicated that the challenge required rowing and that was certainly not their forte. The aim was to travel through the creek, grabbing items from overhead and then pick up the tribal banner before freeing their bound tribe mate who then had to raise the banner.

Things immediately got off to a terrible start for South when within five yards of the start they became beached on a mud bank. Even this slip was not put down to poor navigation:

Lee chooses to blame the local man who gave them a push off, claiming he pushed them into the bank. TV replays fail to bear out this claim. From then on, they weren't so much behind the pace as static. Meanwhile, North had developed a rhythm, and cruised ahead, Alastair at the helm as was becoming normal. According to Alastair, this stability was only achieved by telling Tayfun, who was in the front of the vessel, to stop talking.

"We decided I would steer because I am a senior canoe instructor and the most important thing from my perspective was the steering," he says. "Helen had canoed before and it was agreed among them that anything I said would go. If I said 'in with the paddles' then it happened; the reason it was agreed like that was because of Tay. He had the habit of asking the dumbest questions and when someone said something in the back he would put his oar down and turn around to see what was being said, and the canoe would go over. We'd formulated this to make sure he sat still in the boat at the front. That's the reason we did it. Basically, we just thought he was going to f**k up. I controlled the boat and we got everything and they sank. They panicked and tried to catch up and Lee sank their boat somehow and they were pissed off with him. We ended up rescuing Drew and started paddling and we were petrified it would overturn. Meeta shouted something from the front and Tay tried to tell us and he stopped and turned around, putting us out of sync and he had three people yelling 'Shut up' at him simultaneously. He then really took the hump with us and said, 'Don't tell me to shut up!' In retrospect we were harsh on him but we were petrified that we were going to go over."

Whatever inconveniences North suffered paled in comparison with the travails of South. After extricating themselves from the mudbank, they then got caught up on the opposite bank and then drifted away from the banner. Lee decided to be proactive and jumped in the creek to grab the banner himself.

On his return, however, he capsized the boat, another in the list of small mistakes he was making. John, in particular, was unhappy about Lee's decision, calling it "unwise". It did not matter anyway because by that time North had finished while poor Bridget remained tied to a post upstream. Eventually, South gave up on their hated boat and swam to Bridget, some ten minutes after North had finished. Despite the challenge being lost, Bridget still asked if she could raise the banner aloft and did so. North won some tins of food, a razor (which they tried to hide from Tayfun, for fear he would monopolize it) a wok, shampoo, a single communal toothbrush – much to Tayfun's horror – and some other goods that would help with life on the island. Feeling that luck and everything else was against them, South went back to their camp disconsolate, wet and hungry. They consoled themselves with the thought that it was the next day's Immunity Challenge that was the important one to win – and it was certain not to involve a canoe.

That night, North enjoyed their extra rations while South waited for the next day like condemned men. They did not want to go to Tribal Council a second time because, although the last time had been relatively stress free, if they went again there was certain to be blood on the palm fronds. Neither knew it, in particular Bridget, who had already told cameras "there are no alliances in our tribe" when the air was thick with intrigue, but she or Lee were the two in line if they should lose once more. Bridget is not a political animal by any stretch and was loath to get involved in any backstabbing. Later on, she simply wanted to be told when her time was up so she could prepare for it. Lee was being political, slightly too overtly for many tastes, but he felt confident that he had Susannah's word and he would survive the consequences of the next challenge. John, meanwhile, was gearing himself up to reveal that he was an ex-commando. He cleaned his teeth with ash from the fire, as if to prompt someone to ask what he was doing. But they ignored him, as if it were an everyday occurrence.

One person who was certain he would be leaving if his tribe lost was Tayfun. He was feeling increasingly distant from his tribe mates, claiming that Alastair had turned the girls into his own private harem while Dave acted as his ever-willing henchman. "I don't think it was Al's motivation to create a harem of women with Dave as his sidekick, but that's what he achieved," he says. "Alastair's strategy was the same as mine: to keep a low profile. After he had asserted himself, he said, 'I can't believe what I've done' because he saw that the other tribe had seen that. He had made himself the big leader of our tribe, the big target. He would be the first target for them. I was trying to be quiet and Alastair was falling into the trap that I was trying to avoid. That was because of the mix of personalities we had; six was a nightmare for me because there was not enough room for manoeuvre. My strategy involved having a male on my side – I thought that was important because if I bonded with the girls then that would piss the guys off. I wanted that person to be Alastair. Then I wanted a girl, someone who was very unpopular, that nobody liked, and to be honest that person was Drew. Ideally, it would have been those two and me as a threesome."

Tayfun had only managed to create an alliance of one by day six and he needed his tribe to win. The Immunity Challenge was "Hanging Around". It involved a bar suspended above the water, from which the contestants had to hang for as long as possible. One member from each tribe went head-to-head and the tribe with the longest cumulative time was the winner. This favoured those that were strong yet did not carry too much body weight: in short, John. He decided to go last, to make up any lost time. There was time to make up as well, after Drew held on for a staggering 1 minute 52 seconds, showing just how strong and fit she was. South suffered a blow when Jonny, attempting to adjust his grip, fell in, while Lee was beaten by Dave, to the Newcastle man's utter delight. "I beat the bloody cockney,' he says now, a beam spread across his face, living proof that the north-south divide is as strong as ever. Bridget's doughty performance kept South within touching distance though, but she spoiled it by rather ungraciously shouting "drop, drop!" at the opposition.

The last pair were Tayfun and John. When Tayfun lasted just 50 seconds, John had to hang on for an additional 62 seconds to win, a feat well within his capabilities. When he heard the sound of Tayfun splashing into the water, his eyes opened and a look of delight spread across his face, like a six-year-old set loose in a sweet shop. To the disbelief of the rest of his tribe, John began to show off. He is the sort of man who likes people to know how good he is at things. "We've won this," he called out, smugness writ large across his face. Then he started to do pull-ups, smiling arrogantly, playing the fool. Bridget and Susannah began to count him down; it all looked settled. Then, the results of his showboating began to strike, as lactic acid began to build up in his arms. The look of delight altered to one of concern. His strength started to ebb and as he got nearer to the 1 minute 3 seconds needed to win he became increasingly frantic, scrabbling to stay on to the bar like a gout-ridden budgie trying to stay on its perch. As the end of the countdown got nearer, he lost strength and fell in, emerging to complete silence and a look of downright hostility from Lee. Mark revealed that North had won by seven seconds. Ironically, Bridget and Susannah had counted too slowly and, had John known there were only seven seconds left, he might have summoned the stamina from somewhere to cling on. But the fact remains that he made a complete and utter fool out of himself in front of his tribe, the opposition – and millions of viewers.

"Tayfun lasted about six seconds," he remembers. "It was

really easy and even though I'm not the fittest or strongest it was something I could eminently do. I could have hung there for five minutes, had I just hung on. I'm a bit of a show-off and I like to show people how good I am at things. It was a combination of thinking how good I was at the game and people seeing how strong I was on television. The biggest thing though was that I was just so chuffed that we were going to win and we didn't have to vote someone off. I was just so elated at the prospect of winning that I couldn't contain myself. I felt fine after the pull-ups. Suddenly, the lactic acid built up and there was nothing left. I looked up and saw my forearm shaking and I thought, 'You're going to look a complete prat.' When I fell off I just wanted to swim underwater all the way back to England or just drown. When I got off it was silent, I felt so stupid. I could see the production staff laughing. No one had to say anything because I knew how stupid I had been. It was horrendous. Lee was so furious that he couldn't look at me. He never said anything to me – he couldn't – and I thought that was it. I was really concerned but then part of me wanted to go because I thought I deserved it. Jonny told me it made no difference, somebody had to go and it made no sense to get rid of somebody fit."

Lee's view was somewhat different, though his anger is tempered by disappointment at the performance he put in. "At first when I saw him showboating, I thought, 'What are you doing?' But then it came to me if he was doing that then he must be confident about winning and comfortable. I believed in him. Then I saw the panic set in his eyes, his arms started to quiver. When he fell I knew it wasn't long enough. It was ridiculous. He was an absolute plum."

But more importantly for the way the tribe would vote the next evening were the views of Susannah and Bridget. Susannah's first reaction was relief – that someone else had screwed up besides her. She also noted how furious Lee was afterwards and that meant her view on whose alliance she would like to be in had not altered. Bridget was also more struck by Lee's reaction than any doubts about John. Her view was that he had been stupid, but he knew that and he was better around the camp, whereas Lee was fussy about what he ate. But she did not want to think about who to vote off; it upset her too much, she said, though she had been approached and told they would be voting Lee off and she seemed to accept it, which made her later comments to John about not wanting to talk about who she would vote off a bit disingenuous. Returning to camp, South Island were extremely low, knowing they had to vote one of their number off. At this stage things were looking bad as John admits. "At 6-4 we were a bit down. I was thinking, 'Here we are, TV game show and we're going to look stupid. I'd thought we'd end up 6-2 in the merger. I kept thinking it would be Jonny, Susannah and North Island. I would have placed money on Alastair winning."

For North there were few worries; Tayfun was safe for at least three more days. Back at their camp they could not believe how stupid and arrogant John had been. It coloured their opinion of him a great deal. As Tayfun pointed out, showboating comes when you win, not when you are about to win. Their good mood was affected, however, by the realisation that the awful weather was causing the sea to rise and that their camp was being threatened by the rising tide. North Island was being eaten away. They named it "Sugarcube Island" because it kept dissolving, disappearing. The weather conditions were to worsen, as would the state of North's beach.

It was a long night for their rivals and a galling one. They had lost two Immunity Challenges as a result of two stupid errors. Had they been more careful and disciplined then North Island would be in their position. That night they sat around the fire chatting away, about their favourite films, books and records. Lee felt out of place. John, Jonny and Susannah started discussing how pretty the shape of the log was in the fire. This was not Lee's chosen topic of conversation. "It's a bloody log – get a grip," he thought. Even though he marked Susannah down as a bit pretentious he still felt their alliance was strong, though it had been nagging at the back of his mind that the two Johns might have attempted to lure her into their alliance.

The next day, day seven, was tense, as Susannah tried to decide with John and Jonny whether they should vote off Bridget or Lee, while reassuring Lee that their alliance was still strong. She managed both adroitly. But something even more significant took place that day, off camera. She and Jonny forged an alliance in which, so Susannah believed, they promised to take each other through to the last two if they ever reached that stage. Susannah's period had started while at the beach and she said she was returning to camp. Jonny offered to return with her and the two started talking about how badly things were going. Then one of the defining moments in the game occurred.

"Jonny said to me, 'Who would you prefer to be with out of our three?'" is the way Susannah remembers the encounter. "He was convinced I would say John; but I said him. He said, 'That's fantastic because I would take you through as well.' At that point, we made what I consider to be a really firm agreement that, in the situation of the three of us having to vote against each other, he and I would take each other through. That was something we decided at that point. I got on better with Jonny than John because it took John a week to come out of himself. He was quite uptight at times. He relaxed far more when we were a four. When we walked back to the shelter it was because my period had started on the beach and Jonny said, 'Would you like somebody to come with you?' I thought that was really nice and we had a really, easy, free relaxed discussion and we formed our little pact."

Susannah believed Jonny was to be trusted. He recollects the deal being made but claims it was for purely selfish reasons and that he never intended to see it through because he never expected Susannah to see it through. "My aim was not to be the first one off and to at least reach the jury, if I could not reach the final four. Once we lost the second Immunity Challenge I was worried that I might not even make the jury. That was my aim at that stage, my ultimate aim. She came across to me and we had worked out there would be four Immunity Challenges before the merger. If North Island won them all then we would be down to two people. I thought there was no way I could win it so my aim was to make the jury. Susannah said the way it was going it would be 6-2 and said, 'That two would be you and John, eh?' I did not want to burn my bridges. I wanted to be as friendly with as many people as possible. She said she wouldn't vote against me. But I didn't trust her at all. There was just something about her. She seemed very ambitious. It was nothing she said, just a gut feeling. She's not happy just being a teacher; it seemed clear she had come out to win it, pure and simple. I said 'Yes' and said I wouldn't vote against her. But I didn't think it was serious. There was no way I would have voted against John, even at that time."

John trusted Jonny. He knew that he got on with Susannah very well and while, initially, he was worried about her joining their alliance he never thought Jonny would go against him. "I was against bringing Susannah in to begin with, even though it made sense. I didn't quite trust her from the start. Jonny said he did and they were closer than I was with her – ultimately that was my downfall. They were much closer. Jonny gets on with everyone, even though he may slag people off in the shelter in private, superficially he gets on with everyone. She was quite flirtatious with him, and him with her, I dare say. But she didn't flirt with me. For a start, she was about a foot and a half taller than me so the romantic moment was lost. There was definitely some sort of frisson between them, but then he got on well with all the girls.

"In fact he got on with everybody. He's a chancer like that – very charming and clever. He told me at the start that the main skill he brought there was the fact he was in court a lot, so he talks to judges, lawyers and also he's a drug informant handler, so he has to talk to addicts. He can talk to a spread of people. He would chat to me about legal changes, quite erudite, yet he would talk to Lee about shagging birds and all that. He was a social chameleon. But we got on really, really well from the start. His humour is quite nasty and usually at other people's expense, slagging them off in private. My God, if some of them had heard what he'd said they'd have never voted for him at the end. We were both like that. Our humour was quite similar."

The decision still had to be made about whom to vote off that evening. Lee was the stronger and fitter, on paper at least, while Bridget was very useful around the camp in the mother role, such as cooking, tending the fire. Every morning she was the first up and by the time other people were wiping the sleep from their eyes, a roaring fire would be on the go. Bridget had also been very determined in the challenges and had showed fight and grit, always doing better than expected. The same could not be said for Lee during "Hanging Around". Bridget and Susannah also had a subject in common: it turned out that they both supported the same charity, ABC – Action against Breast Cancer. For these reasons, so they claim, the three decided to vote off Lee. The fact is he did not fit in to their clique as well as Bridget, who had her uses in their eyes, and he was political, capable of forming alliances and upsetting their gameplan. He did not join in their discussions about the shape of the clouds or favourite Shakespearean sonnets. He was overtly scheming and ambitious. On the other hand, Bridget could be relied on to do nothing in that department and was therefore, as she admitted, "a pawn in this game". She would be sacrificed when the time was right.

Before walking in to Tribal Council, Lee asked Susannah one more time if their alliance was still strong and said she convinced him it was. "She stared me in the eye, cold as you like, and said we were together five minutes before we got there I can't understand why she did that, because at that point there was no need to go that far and lie so blatantly. It's not as if I had time to do anything about it. I liked her; she made me laugh. But she's a very, very good liar."

At Tribal Council, it turned out to be quite different and he walked off in a daze, but not so surprised that he did not find time to shoot a look in the direction of Susannah who had, he said later, "done me like a kipper". It had the desired effect: Susannah felt awful. "He turned around and looked at me and it was daggers. I felt really bad, really awful. After that, I did not want to do it again. From that point on I decided I wanted to play the game as straight as I could and not lie to anyone, particularly with people I had been honest with and who I really respected." This boded well for Jonny, not that he would have believed Susannah had she told him.

That Tribal Council had been an emotional one. Bridget cried but that was hardly news – her tears fell as often as the rain – but more importantly it was cathartic for South Island. They now had a tightly-knit group of four with a range of skills. It could not get worse surely, though some thought it might. That night everyone was upset when they got back, even Jonny. John was appalled at their emotion, complaining how he was worried that he almost got pulled into a group hug. Susannah was trying to console herself by remembering that Lee had told her how much he admired the way that Charlotte had played the game in the first series. She hoped he would understand that she too was just playing the game in voting him off. Sitting around the fire, dejected, they started talking about Alastair's ex-forces background and why someone would want to lie about their past. Susannah said to John, "You're a barrister, I can think of lots of reasons why you might lie about that." John nervously and quietly replied, "Would you reveal you had a forces background?" No one picked up on it. John bottled out of telling them. His hints were being ignored. It seemed only an outright confession would do.

Lee took his dismissal in good spirit. He knew it was part of the game but he could not hide his disappointment. He has no hard feelings towards his tribe but he won't be inviting them over for Sunday lunch. He feels he would have got on better with the other tribe – this is ironic given the dislike Dave had for him, but perhaps that had been stirred up by the ever-manipulative Alastair? It is a purely academic thought but a consoling one for someone who had such ambitions and wanted to go as far as he could. Being voted off second was extremely disappointing for him. Still, it did change his life in one way: when he returned he decided he could not face his old job so he left and is casting around for a new challenge. He also learned that he could go without food, something he never, ever thought would be the case before he travelled out to Panama.

"I've never been camping before – I'm probably the male version of Sarah. Friends and family didn't think I'd be able to handle the lifestyle, living rough and the problem with the food. They said, 'You'll never last without eating' because obviously I do like my food. I deliberately put on a stone before I went, which was hardly tough. I will never ever eat coconut again – just the thought of it makes me feel sick. It's like when you're young and you got drunk on a drink and you feel so bad afterwards that you can never drink it again. That's how I feel about coconut. Food was my biggest fear but I actually surprised myself. When I get hungry the colour fades from my face and I get really bad-tempered so I was worried about what would happen on the island. It wasn't that bad though. At one stage I didn't eat for three days and I coped with it surprisingly well."

Stand by Your Tribe

The crows on North Island had a narrow escape. Drew, who was emerging from her wallflower stage and becoming a valued member of her tribe, growing in confidence with each day, decided that crows would be a good source of protein. On day eight she tried to build a net that would catch birds, though it proved unsuccessful. The net around Tayfun, however, was closing by the day and he knew it. He was in a frustrating position, being able to see through Alastair's strategy but not being able to say anything because, given how close-knit the group was, it would have backfired and even hastened his demise. On the other hand, his attempts to ingratiate himself with Alastair were failing, and he was making little headway among the women. It was fanciful of him to think he could worm his way into the affections of Dave and Alastair: "big girl's blouse", "fanny" and "jessie" were just some of the colourful phrases they had used to describe him. Both Dave, a married man with two sons, and Alastair, a confirmed bachelor, are traditional, unreconstructed males who believed in hard graft and men being men. Even though Tayfun is not gay, Dave and Alastair certainly thought he was.

By day eight, Dave was particularly fed up with the dancer. "I thought I might have a problem with the dickhead who threw the machete in the water but he turned out to be a canny lad. He was hopeless, though, terrible. I thought he was a plant by the production company at first. He was a professional dancer, no hair on his body at all. I thought 'Aye, aye.' It didn't bother us, but what a wimp! One day, we were building the shelter and we were getting the palm leaves for the roof and Alastair and me were building the frame, tying things up. Sand was everywhere but what do you expect when you're on a beach? I says to Tayfun, 'Give us a hand. Put another leaf on and I'll tie it. Just guide it up from the inside.' He went in and I put it on and some sand fell on him. Not much mind. But he went 'Oh!' I said 'What's wrong?' I thought he'd hurt himself. And he was slapping himself and dancing around. He says, 'Something's on me.' I says, 'It's f***ing sand man. It just fell off the leaf, that's all.' I thought then and there: 'This kid's going to be a joy.' When I voted him off I said 'Tay, you're a canny lad but if you helped others like you help yourself, your life would be different.' He'd have been all right on *Millionaire* with Tarrant because he was dead intelligent. But he had no common bloody sense at all."

The "he's a nice lad but …" comment might be extremely patronising but it was the view that all the tribe had reached. Alastair was the one person who might have let Tayfun back into the group but that was never going to happen. Instead, Tayfun was isolated from Alastair and Dave and was forced to seek solace with the women. "He was so different," remembers Alastair. "One example: Dave and I were doing a lot of stuff and we were accused of not including Tay in things. The reason we didn't do that was because it was easier to do it ourselves. I was making a bench and wanted to move it away from the water so

I asked Tay to give me a hand lifting it. It was a 20-second job and he said, 'I'll have to go and get changed.' I thought, 'I'll just do it myself.' It is not because we disliked him, it was just that it was easier to do it ourselves. From that moment on he would go off by himself; he isolated himself. There was an axe incident when I was chopping and I thought to give him a go and he did it pathetically. He was a complete wuss, but I mean that in an affectionate way."

This comment is classic Alastair; an insult dressed as a compliment. A charismatic man, whose size gives him great physical presence, he can do nothing but lead, even though he claims he was not leader of North Island and was more a "facilitator". But his style did not grate with the others, though a few did grow weary of his incessant stream of stories about his personal life and achievements, that seemed to go on and on with little point to them. Even though he has a dominant, forceful personality, Alastair's aim was to try and remain in the background; play the "Grey Man". He was incapable of doing that, or keeping quiet about his ex-forces background, which he admitted to early on – though he kept up the pretence of being a fuel cards salesman, which the gullible lot swallowed hook, line and sinker. He did succeed, Tayfun aside, in bringing North Island together to form a formidable unit. In fact, such was the warmth and friendship among North Island that it became nauseating, all the mutual backslapping and encouragement. Watching them on occasions, one yearned for some good old-fashioned bitchiness. Luckily, Tayfun was willing to supply it when interviewed back in London for this book. He is particularly angry about the reverse snobbery he felt he suffered from.

"Alastair used the northern element. There was a Sheffield lass, a Geordie and him, Scottish, and they all have these really broad accents. He alienated me because of the way I spoke. He was making me out as some sort of colonial. He was going on about how they had strong regional accents and he kept telling the others, 'I love your accent, I love your accent.' They used that accent thing and bonded.

"He said he had been in the RAF, been to university and worked for some fuel company. Basically, the guy stank of bullshit the whole time. I could hear him speak all this crap but you can't say anything because that gives them reason to turn against you. I could not say anything because I was trying to reintegrate myself into the tribe. To me, Alastair was a lot more successful at what he does than he lets on. He was almost applying textbook sales techniques on people. I found it cheesy and corny but my tribe seemed really gullible. He is a natural leader and when you are big as he is and in an environment like that, it is an asset. He was a big action man, good at motivating and a smart guy. He had a lot of strengths. He is very savvy. To me, however, he was like a dodgy used car salesman, always giving the pitch to people, flattering them. I felt he was very condescending, particularly with Dave. When he was hanging on the bars, ("Hanging Around") he kept telling him there would be a framed photograph of him in the pub, saying 'You'll be the local hero beating a man half your age.' He kept repeating these messages to people. You could see Dave's chest swell. I felt like saying to him, 'Dave, there's a million pounds up for grabs. Can't you see what he's doing?' I found him creepy and manipulative. But he was playing the game bloody well, so fair play to him. I'm still not sure about his strategy – it was all short term, up until the merger and he had not looked beyond that at all."

Tayfun, realising that he was out of luck with the men, although he made a last-ditch offer to Alastair in an attempt to save himself, was also out of luck with the females, who did not view him any differently. His overriding interest in his own cleanliness and wellbeing marked him out to be selfish, his attempts at politics went down badly with a tribe that had basically banned all talk of alliances until post-merger, and they too isolated him. "Tayfun is a lovely guy," says Meeta, who probably got on best with him out of them all. "He's very intelligent and switched on. But everyone got cheesed off with him being such a big girl's blouse. Tayfun would take an hour to get ready for bed; making sure he had no creases, doing his hair. If a fly landed on him he went mad. He was more worried about what he looked like rather than helping around the camp. There's nothing wrong in taking pride in what you look like, and he's a nice-looking bloke, but it wasn't the right place for that. He stood around while the lads dug trenches. He wouldn't carry the water and he'd complain that his shoulder was hurting. We all did that sort of thing, collecting firewood and shelter. We won an axe and he had the axe to find some leaves and if he found a cobweb he'd stop and walk around it to avoid it. He just wasn't cut out for island life." As someone not cut out herself, Meeta knew what she was talking about.

As a final strategy Tayfun tried to appeal to the group as a whole, trying to prompt debates about the world, current affairs and, on one memorable occasion, religion. Musing on the Holy Cross, he wondered out loud about how odd it was that Christians use as a symbol of religion the very apparatus used to crucify their saviour. If he had been beheaded by guillotine, he wondered further, would people wear guillotines around their necks? It is a debate that has fascinated people since time immemorial and minds greater than Tayfun's have thought upon it. But it was of no interest to North Island. "Tayfun, why do you talk a load of sh*te," was Helen's response to this piece of theological argument, before switching the subject to something more profound, like what sort of chocolate cake she would like to eat or informing everyone on the regularity of her bowel movements. ("I've just had a right good sh*t," became Helen's catchphrase.) Then Alastair struck up a similar refrain: "I once knew this girl/bloke/goldfish …," and people would listen as he rambled on interminably. Tayfun just did not fit. North was an alliance of five. Tayfun's time was running out.

The end was brought nearer when South brought their losing streak to a close at the Fast Fire Challenge. Before it started, Dave noticed that South had voted Lee off. This surprised North, who had thought it would be Bridget, and Dave gave the lads the thumbs up about their choice. The Reward Challenge involved melting a block of ice containing a tribal flag and a leg of lamb. The first to melt the ice and raise the flag above their fire won the challenge. Before the challenge, South asked if they could roll the ice into the sea, an idea of Bridget's, though Susannah bridles somewhat at that suggestion, claiming she came up with the idea, as she was used to defrosting fillet mignon in her Wimbledon kitchen by using warm water. Ed Forsdick said that was OK and on hearing that, North did the same. However, they failed to grasp the concept and kept the block in one place while trying to defrost it, so the water around it went cold. For South, Jonny kept rolling it to fresh warm water and rubbed it vigorously with gloves, holding it between his thighs – leading to jokes about his "hot thighs" later on. As a consequence, their block melted far quicker than the opposition's and they were first to raise their flag above the fire. Alastair made a few noises about their block being larger than South's but this was discounted. (In fact, both blocks were made in the same mould.) The prize was a fresh leg of lamb and some fishing gear. South were up and running at last.

Their mood before leaving camp that morning had been

listless; that afternoon they were jubilant. John joked that they won because he had nothing to do with tactics, while Bridget, in her element, cooked the lamb. Not one morsel was wasted; they ate the meat, sucked and gnawed the bones and then boiled them to make stock. Watching them sit around the fire sucking bones had a vaguely cannibalistic air but they were very happy. They had the sense that as a four they were a lot more united than they had been before; Bridget's bright idea also showed the value of keeping her instead of Lee because it was doubtful that he would have thought up the same plan. Their full bellies and the smell of fried lamb wafting around the camp meant that even the incessant rain failed to douse their burgeoning sense of optimism. They felt they had made the first step towards avoiding a rout and getting themselves back in the game and Bridget felt far more secure.

"The elation was immense after winning that reward," she says. "The other three in the tribe also instantly recognised that getting rid of Lee was the best thing they did. I built the fire, while Jonny rolled around the ice and John and Susannah collected wood. Everyone knew their position and what they had to do and it worked perfectly. It felt good because rolling the block into the sea was my idea and it worked. But even though we won John told us not to get carried away because there could be a twist in the tail. Ed was a bit cheesed off that we didn't celebrate. Before the next challenge, Ed said 'If you finish first then you will celebrate.' "

That night, as South tried to think of another use for lamb bones, North had a game of charades, prompted by Tayfun. He missed a chance to make Dave reconsider his negative attitude towards dancing by performing "Billy Elliot", but on the whole the game was a success. As he remembers it, "it went down well because every night listening to Alastair's stories was terrible; he would just drone on and on and on about these bloody boring subjects – usually himself." But it would take a bit more than a lively game of charades to save his skin. Instead, it needed North to win immunity.

It was a stormy night and the next morning, day nine, a huge wave hit North's camp and they were forced to re-evaluate the position of their camp. They decided to reinforce the wall to stop the waves reclaiming the camp and started to work, Tayfun included, though he kept going into the sea to wash his hands. He admits to wanting to keep clean and doesn't see why that's a problem, though it was foolish of him to think this would not mark him out as different. As for being selfish, he claims he was trying to save himself. "They created this work ethic and I thought we should conserve energy for the challenges, the most important aspect. All the others were looking for jobs they could do. It was if they were socially inadequate and could not sit down and relax and have proper discussions and debate. I just wanted to do what I needed to do and what the tribe really needed; it was nothing about not wanting to get dirty. Admittedly, they weren't the most hygienic people I had ever met in my life but I think they were just looking for excuses to get rid of me and anything they could find was a reason. The lads just did not want me there."

Tayfun was also concerned when he saw that Lee had been voted off because it meant that North could afford to lose a man and not feel at a disadvantage, though so little did they rate Tayfun's strength that they still might have persisted with voting him off even if Lee had not gone. He comforted himself with the thought that Meeta had made it abundantly clear that she wanted to be voted off when they lost an Immunity Challenge. He underestimated, however, the desire to see him go, particularly from Dave, which is ironic considering how fulsome Tayfun is when he speaks of the Geordie. Tayfun had trials with Manchester City and likes football and he thought he could get along with Dave on a "macho" level. Unfortunately, Dave thought Tayfun was as macho as a vicar in a tutu.

The next Immunity Challenge therefore was vital for Tayfun and for South Island, who knew they had to win to have any chance of going into merger on level terms and so avoid being picked off one by one. The challenge was to be a swimming relay. The idea had been for each tribe to be chained together and at different stages they would have to drop a tribe member, but the currents caused by the weather made it too dangerous to have people shackled together. So a relay was devised instead, involving each tribe member – minus Meeta and Helen from North to balance numbers – having to swim under two obstacles and then pick up a conch shell, which they then had to bring back a starting position and place in a bowl before the next swimmer could enter the water. North's problem was Dave, who only had one pair of glasses with him which he did not want to lose, so he did not wear them. Spotting the conch might prove a problem. Dave kicked up a fuss, claiming the challenge discriminated against him, a view backed vociferously by the other contestants. Already, the whingeing and whining had begun, an unappealing characteristic of several contestants. Was Dave's claim to be half-blind merely a tactic to make him appear a pathetic old man and therefore not a threat, or was it perhaps a way to get his excuses in early should hefoul up the challenge? The former theory is borne out by the excellent show he made in later challenges, such as the Spider Cave, where he managed to find a number of tiny spiders in the pitch dark without any trouble, or, more pointedly, when he won the only challenge that really required good eyesight, Ever Decreasing Targets.

As it turned out, in this challenge Dave found the conch without problems but was slow through the obstacles. South turned out to be far stronger swimmers than their counterparts in the North Island, with the notable exception of Alastair, a former senior water polo player for Scotland, who almost pulled back a massive deficit to win with an astonishing performance. Even the underwater cameramen were impressed. He did cut himself in a tender place, however, transporting the conch in his trunks. Only three seconds were in it by the end, but to their joy South had finally won the immunity idol. Delighted, they returned and placed it lovingly on the mantelpiece they had created.

It was bad news for Tayfun. It got worse when Meeta suddenly said she did not want to go home yet and that she could last a few days more. It crossed Tayfun's mind that this was more than convenient for his tribe because they could get rid of him and then Meeta whenever they wished, keeping their cosy foursome intact. He casts doubt on Meeta's claim that she wanted to go home because it was so tough and the weather was so bad. In his view she did not want the humiliation of being voted off so she headed her tribe off at the pass by asking to go. He is wrong though; Meeta was truly unhappy and wanted to leave. She was so homesick that every time she saw the producer who filmed her at home before the game started, Dean Palmer, she just burst into tears because it reminded of her home. Pathetic it may be, but it was genuine. After losing that challenge she thought she was going and was subsequently delighted. But then Alastair approached her. "He came up to me and said, 'You're not going anywhere.' I said, 'What do you mean?' He said, 'Tayfun is going. Regardless of whether we lose immunity or rewards by not having him there, we just want him out.' "

That evening Tayfun attempted to spread disharmony among the group by introducing controversy. He was heartily sick of the superficial chumminess of his group. "Everyone was pretending to be so nice and so friendly and they kept going on about having such a good team spirit and that's why we've been winning, which was rubbish because we only won because they made two errors and then they beat us and it was us that were the absolutely useless team. Had they got their act together earlier it would have been us 6-3 down and with no chance of winning another challenge. I wasn't into this 'we're a really great team' thing. I wanted to expose people more; get them to be more open about who they were and what they thought, by picking controversial topics for discussion that I thought people would form strong opinions about one way or the other. Knowing that Drew and Helen would have strong views on feminism, while Dave was traditional and old, I thought that this would work. Alastair was quite traditional but he drove me mad, sitting on the fence, 'I see what you're saying, I appreciate your view and that's a good point, but I also see what you're saying is very true.' This was even though they were two very opposite opinions."

First, he initiated a debate about feminism and whether women should stay at home to look after kids or not. Drew and Helen both agreed it was down to the individual woman to decide while Meeta differed in typically forthright fashion. "My opinion is that if you can't look after and be with your child then you shouldn't have one. Why bother if you are going to get someone else to look after your kid? If you want a career then don't open your legs; simple as that." Alastair then took control of the discussion, asking whether it was fair that parents who could afford it should work and leave their child with a nanny. He said that if any woman he wanted to marry categorically said she would want to work afterwards and get a nanny, then he would have doubts about her. From other people's answers, he deduced that other people thought it wasn't right for parents to foist their child on a nanny, but Helen and Drew said they still wanted the option, which he agreed with. This long interruption cleverly took the sting out of Tayfun's original question. So he chose another subject: gynaecologists. Tayfun said that if he was female he would have a problem with seeing a male gynaecologist because "he obviously has an expressed interest in female genitalia". Dave then went to bed. And who could blame him? Tayfun's choice of subject might have gone down well at the Cambridge Free Press over a white wine spritzer after a lively meeting of the Debating Society but to this lot it seemed just plain weird.

The next morning people's feelings had hardened towards Tayfun. Dave claims he found in Tayfun's bag some anti-itching cream which he had got from the medics for the many bites he had received. He kept this from the others and they were upset because they had all been bitten to shreds. Tayfun saw how things were shaping up and decided to approach Alastair a final time to try and cut a deal. "At the eleventh hour Tay came to me and tried to make a deal," Alastair recounts. "He assumed I was leading the others and it was an assumption that I was annoyed at and so were the others when I told them. He said, 'If you don't vote me off I promise I will support you and at merger I will vote for you and I'll be your undying supporter.' I said, 'To be honest you're talking to the wrong person. I don't know what I'm going to do' – which was a lie – 'and the others are all intelligent, free-thinking people who will make their own decisions.' That was a lie because we had already decided but perhaps I didn't want to face reality or a confrontation. He had pestered us all day. Then he made a comment later, saying 'Very intelligent, Alastair. The minute I told you that you went and told everybody else to put them against me.' I said, 'Tay, I did tell them but that wasn't going to make any difference because they had made their decision.' "

Tayfun made it clear to the two men that he believed they were stupid to go forward with three women because when the time came they would gang up and vote the pair of them off. Predictably, this made its way back to the girls and another wedge was driven between Tayfun and the group. Helen was particularly incensed, referring to Tayfun as an "arsehole" and saying that him not being used to the environment "was no excuse for him trying to bitch and backstab". This is a staggering comment. What did she expect Tayfun to do? Nobly accept his fate and wander off into the sunset? No, in his own words, he wanted to go down "kicking and screaming" even though he could tell by people's reaction to him that day that he was doomed.

"Drew had been a miserable woman until that last day, throughout the whole time she had this permanent scowl on her face, and she was always moaning and whinging. 'I'm tired of being filmed' or 'Can't they (the cameramen) go away and leave me?' I was thinking, 'This is a TV programme, love.' I thought she had no sense of fun. On that last day she was really nice to me, and she had never done that. I thought, 'Aye, aye, you're voting me off.' In contrast, Helen was completely incapable of looking me in the eye. I got on very well with her to begin with; she was very sweet to me, but Alastair got to her. I did not want to flirt with the girls because I thought, 'If you flirt with one girl then you can cheese the others off. The blokes can get annoyed as well.' But then Alastair went and flirted very strongly with Helen and they bonded. He was flattering her like mad and she appreciated it."

That evening was North's first visit to Tribal Council and the weather was appalling – so bad that they were unable to return to their beach that evening and had to sleep rough on El Limbo. Tayfun was fully aware that he was going but still decided to vote for Meeta in the hope that Dave and

Alastair would "see common sense" and change their minds. It was not to be and he was the first person to be ejected from North Island.

He was not too upset because he knew he could have gone a lot sooner had they lost an Immunity Challenge earlier. He had made a fool out of himself at the airport, lost the machete – Dave was still complaining about him losing that on day ten! – but his main problem was that he was simply too different. There was little he could have done to compensate for that other than adopt another personality. Drew summed it up when she told the camera that Tayfun did not gel and was the only member of the group that failed to do so. Tayfun, however, cannot believe that Drew had the front to say that. "I couldn't believe it when she said I was the one person who didn't gel and fit in with the tribe because I can hear people saying that about Drew in life," was his reaction.

He is quite gracious about the people who ostracised him, however. He says Helen is a "remarkable girl". "She is very with it, very together and her head is very much screwed on. She is strong-minded and determined. She is the sort of person that, if she sets her mind to do something, then she will achieve it. But she does lack natural exuberance; there is no sense of mischief or playfulness there. She said that if she won she would knock down the council house wall that divided her parents and next door, after buying it, and make one big house. I thought, 'Is that what you would do with a million pounds? Utterly bizarre.' " This is a subject that gave John and Jonny some amusement later.

"Drew is quite a sporty woman, strong and determined, especially when competing against men. I admire that attitude totally. The only problem was her whining. Meeta I adored, she was good fun. Dave is the man I would like to have won it; I really liked him. Alastair's tactics were bad, I think – I don't see how he could win the way he was playing the game. He's a cheesy salesman, completely full of crap. I would never buy a thing from him – he's only comfortable with people he was superior to. He was not comfortable with me."

"You Looking at Me?"

South Island were coming together. Around the time of their second Immunity Challenge defeat, they looked as if they might be routed. Only Jonny had any real energy and was coping with the deprivations, while John in particular was becoming weak: having no fat stores to lose, he started losing muscle. His natural good humour was also ebbing somewhat. But the "Fire and Ice" Reward Challenge had given them strength and hope and the subsequent Immunity Challenge had given them time to take stock, rather than worry about whom they would vote off next. In particular, John was coming out of himself, cracking jokes at people's expense and trading quips with Jonny. The pair were becoming great friends. It transpired they shared a birthday, November 23, though John is a year older and it was difficult to see what, if anything, would break them. They knew the merger would be coming soon and that, even if they lost the next Immunity Challenge, then Bridget would go. This was hard on Bridget and the realisation that she was expendable was difficult to accept, given how much she valued her "mother" role in the tribe. On day ten she was in tears (again). She felt segregated, cut off and was starting to miss her real kids. Bridget also differed in that she is rural and loves the countryside, having only been to London once before her interviews for *Survivor*. She is also intensely patriotic – hence the Union Jack thong – right-wing and "old-fashioned" in her views on sexuality and race. This isolated her from her left-leaning, urbane professional, city-dwelling tribe mates.

One story sums up the difference and explains some of the

later irritation the boys in particular came to feel for Bridget. While they were sitting round the fire, the conversation turned to the tragedy of September 11. As they discussed the horrendous images of that day, Bridget immediately piped up and said she had never seen the planes crashing into the World Trade Center. Jonny was incredulous. "What do you mean you never saw that," he asked. "It was on TV constantly for weeks; the world stopped to watch it. It's the most significant thing that has happened in our lifetimes." Bridget shrugged her shoulders. "It didn't affect me. I didn't know anybody who was hurt or killed so it doesn't interest me." The others were amazed by what they saw as her ignorance. Then Jonny was astounded that when he mentioned the outbreak of foot-and-mouth disease, Bridget burst into tears when she spoke of a fellow farmer who had been affected. Like Tayfun, Bridget was different and that difference set her apart. But, contrary to Tayfun, Bridget would not attempt to shore up her position; she was simply happy to contribute. They were also wary of her claims to be poor. She inadvertently let slip that she owned a lot of land and that her boyfriend could get nearly a million for his farm if he chose to sell it. Not like a farmer to plead poverty while sitting happily on a huge fat pile of cash. The fact was that the "Hampstead massif" claimed to like her, and still do, but they had a funny way of showing it sometimes. They tolerated her, enjoyed having her there to banter with because she took the ribbing well and she cared for them. Susannah got a bit annoyed that Bridget hogged the "domestic" role, but most of the time they were happy to leave that side of things to her. Despite that, they functioned a lot more equally than North Island, where the women cooked and tidied while the men did the carrying, fetching, digging and building.

Day eleven brought another Reward Challenge, though neither side was too geared up for it after yet another night of torrential, driving rain that prevented much sleep. The challenge was an interesting one; a member of each tribe was to be selected to travel by helicopter on an "Ambassador's Visit" to the other island to find out as much as they could about the other. The rule was that people had to be as truthful as they had been with their own tribe. The question was, who to select to go? On the one hand it could be a bonus, in that the selected person could befriend the other tribe and have an "in" for the merger. However, if it went wrong it could prejudice their chances later. This was the case for Susannah, who was ordered by John and Jonny not to tell North Island that John had a forces background, which he revealed to South Island on the eve of the Reward Challenge, and not to say under any circumstances which members of their tribe had a vote against them. They selected Susannah because they thought that, as a teacher, she would be good at remembering details, having to memorise children's names at work. But the constraints of what she could and felt she could not say proved a problem, as she recollects.

"I was put in quite a difficult position. Before I went over both John and Jonny said, 'Don't tell them anything. Nothing they don't need to know.' So it was a case of how much do you share? John had asked me not to say anything about his Marine background, which he had just confessed to. I had gone over thinking that if Alastair asks me any question about John's Marine background then I've got to get out of it somehow and I also didn't want to tell them who had votes cast against them. We were in an inferior position if those votes counted after merger. So I was going with two things that my tribe were adamant I couldn't disclose and of course they were two of the first things I was asked. We were told to be completely honest and I was put in the position where I was trying to be Miss Diplomat in a way and not say anything but I think it may have made me look quite untrustworthy. Alastair asked,

'Does John have an army background?' I said he was a physiotherapist. It was all really difficult. It gave me an advantage because I met them, but on the other hand I think they thought I was hiding something."

While Dave and Alastair found her charming – a view that would alter as time passed – the girls felt she could not be trusted. Meeta did not like the way Susannah gushed; so that when Drew said she was a firefighter, Susannah would say "Really! Brilliant!" and Meeta thought that was false. "I shampooed her hair for her, thinking she was really nice. She asked Drew what her name was and when she answered she said, 'Lovely'. She just kept saying 'Wow' and 'fantastic' about things that weren't fantastic. She just seemed devious and a bit insincere. I didn't take to her, not in that environment. I mean, she might be a lovely girl but I didn't think so then."

Susannah had also told them they had only been eating rice while Helen discovered that they had also been eating runner beans and limes. Helen, although she herself was on South Island during Susannah's visit, liked her but thought her "devious", for having given up her job teaching to enter *Survivor*. "I wouldn't resign from a job like that. You don't resign from a well-paid job to come here unless you want to win," she added, obviously unaware that teaching in an inner-city London school is hardly the world's best paid and most stress-free job. She had a point though: Susannah was there to win. Unlike Helen, who claimed that her motivation was the experience and she would not compromise her values and principles for the money. This was the standard response from a lot of the competitors, like Dave, Drew and Bridget. All were big admirers of Andy from the last series, who they felt played the game to the best of his ability but was also honourable. He didn't stoop to the others' level and came away without the money but with his dignity and reputation intact.

Drew thought Susannah was too nice. "It was just too much. I don't appreciate people like that. I would just rather people told me they didn't like something or didn't say anything at all than just pretend for the sake of it. I can't respect that. I wouldn't say something nice for the sake of it."

Ironically, on Helen's visit to South Island, when she asked who had votes against them John and Jonny told her straight away, she claims, while Susannah was squirming and wriggling under questioning from North. North now thought they had a massive advantage, knowing John and Bridget had votes against them while only Meeta from their tribe had a vote. Helen might have been able to extract that piece of information but she was not very good at extracting anything else, though everyone found her affable. It is impossible not to. She had volunteered to go because she thought it would be useful in the future to find out all she could about the others. She then shared all the information with her tribe so they could use that information at a later date if she was voted off ahead of them. For the next couple of nights she gave her tribe tutorials on South and all the information she had mustered.

But as the morning progressed, John and Jonny bombarded her with questions deliberately so that she was unable to ask her own. Then they put into place Plan B: Bridget. "She went to speak to Bridget and, as you know, Bridget can talk, and she will talk to anyone who listens. Actually, she'll even speak when you are not listening," Jonny recollects. "She'll go on about her daughters, about everyone in her family, about her oven, her parents' oven, her father's daughter's sister's cousin's pet dog's oven. So we fobbed Helen off on her and it worked because she knew bugger all."

She knew slightly more than that but when it came time for the questions to be asked, she was found wanting. She answered incorrectly that Jonny was the youngest member of

South Island. Mistakenly, Helen believed she only had to find out about the people she met and forgot about Susannah who was on her island at the time. She also forgot that both she and Susannah could play a joker if there was a question either was unsure of. She got the question wrong and the prize went to South – their third victory in a row. It was waiting for them back at the beach – a karaoke machine and some beer with nibbles. The beer lit up everyone's eyes, the karaoke machine less so, apart from John who saw a chance to show off. A few swigs of beer on an empty stomach later, however, and the karaoke began to look increasingly attractive. Before long, they could not be stopped, John leading off with an astonishing Elvis impersonation and then "Take Me Home Country Roads"; Susannah revealing a singing voice so deep that it would shame Barry White on "Fly Me To The Moon"; Bridget massacring "Stand By Your Man"; both performing "Knowing Me, Knowing You". It was on the list but no one chose the apt "Two Tribes" by Frankie Goes to Hollywood. Finally, there was the crowning glory, Jonny and John performing "YMCA" by the Village People, complete with neckerchiefs, poking fun at the dapper presenter, Mark Nicholas. As a result of that performance, they started referring to themselves as the "The Two Gay Jonnies" and John joked with Jonny that he would spark a gay recruitment drive in the police force. "There'll be pictures of you in 'The Pink Plod'," he joked.

They all agreed it was a fantastic night, by far the best on the island so far. Even the incessant rain failed to crush their good mood, the beer seeing to that. Given they had had so little to eat, a couple was all that was required to make them merry. It also cast off any self-conscious worry about making fools of themselves on national TV. They knew it was too late for that. Their morale was high and they intended to keep hold of the immunity idol, to which they had fed crisps and beer as an offering. It had been perfect preparation for the next day.

Ever since arriving on the island the contestants had been expecting an Eating Challenge of some sort after watching last year's contestants having to eat a wriggling grub. They were steeling themselves for the challenge but never in their wildest flights of fancy did they expect what was waiting for them on day twelve. In the morning when they picked up their Treemail people's hearts skipped a beat.

> *It might seem hard to swallow*
> *When you step up to the spinner,*
> *But the things you see are a delicacy*
> *And today will be your dinner.*
>
> *This game is food for thought,*
> *Though it might stick in your throat.*
> *If you refuse you're sure to lose*
> *Your chance to miss the vote.*

Both tribes deduced it would be an Eating Challenge and blew a sigh of relief that former members of their tribe were not there to participate. South were glad that Lee was not involved, given his pickiness about coconut and rice; North claim Tayfun had said he would not be able to eat anything wriggling or revolting if it cropped up. Before leaving, North formulated a plan: Meeta reckoned she could eat almost anything, having, she says, "eaten all sorts" while living in India. Knowing that in the event of a tie it was likely each tribe would be forced to pick the most squeamish member of the other to play-off for immunity at the end, it was decided she would fake her horror. This would take the heat off Drew who was terrified that she would have to eat something that wriggled. On South Island no such plans were hatched but Jonny was easily the most worried, given his fear of spiders. "I'm the sort of bloke that kills them with a hammer when I see them in the bathroom," he says. "I know it's irrational but I just can't stand them."

He knew, however, that this was a crucial challenge, as did all the others. If South were to lose then they would be 5-3 at merger and would almost certainly have been picked off afterwards. If they won, then it would be level. Both tribes had made a pact to stick together after the merger and vote en bloc. One person who had mixed feelings about the challenge was Meeta. She was desperate to go back and see her brother and fiancé and victory in the challenge would make it likely she would go through to the merger and then become a member of the jury. That would mean being involved until the end, which was almost four weeks in the future. The idea of that was unbearable. Yet she had bonded very well with her tribe and wanted one of them to win. Therefore she thought she was willing to give her all in the next challenge even though her heart was not really in it.

The two tribes gathered at Dolphin Bay. On a revolving table sat a number of covered dishes, selected and researched by challenge producer Chris Brogden and researcher Chris Sussman, and tested by some of the local boatmen, none of the crew having been willing to volunteer themselves as guinea pigs. A member of each tribe was to face another across the table and the table was spun. When it stopped they had to eat whatever was in front of them. There were two portions of each "dish" so that both ate the same. Because of the disparity in numbers, a member of South Island had to go twice and that person was John. He went up first against Alastair and their treat was what many regarded as the most repulsive dish: the fish eye, which John said was "the size of a baby's head". Dave, looking on, thought to himself, "How big is the friggin' fish?" John did not react immediately. "I couldn't see what it was I had to eat because normally I wear glasses and I was back from the table and for some reason I thought it was a glass thing of pâté. God knows why. I was about to ask for a few water biscuits. I picked it up and there was cartilage on it as well so it wasn't soft. It was really hard and there was bone. It burst in my mouth and it went down my throat and it was gross. It tasted like the most off fish. I almost puked. Alastair's went out the side of his mouth. It took ages to chew. It was utterly disgusting."

As John noticed, fortunately for Alastair his eye exploded and the gunk flew out of the side of his mouth. He thought he got the best deal too. "I don't how the hell I ate mine because I can't even eat brussels sprouts, never mind fish eyes. John had a bigger eye than me and he spent twice as long chewing it because he couldn't get it down. I tried to swallow mine straight away but it was like a golf ball. It was huge."

Next to the table were Drew and Bridget. The former was desperately trying to keep her composure and hide from South Island the sheer terror she was experiencing. When the table stopped spinning and her meal was revealed, she was delighted to see it was neither alive nor an eyeball. "Had it been something wriggling then I'm not sure if I could have eaten it, I really don't. The beetle was the worst. But I was really, really lucky because the testicle was probably the easiest thing to eat." Few people have ever been so happy to see a testicle. Both she and Bridget made light work of what they ate. When Bridget returned to her tribe and was asked what it tasted like, she was unflinching in her description. "Like someone has come in my mouth," she replied frankly. Not one to stand on ceremony, Bridget.

Dave and Jonny went head to head next and, to the latter's dismay, on his plate was a huge beetle, very much alive and not particularly keen about its participation in *Survivor*. Jonny could not believe it. "I'd said before I wanted something soft, not anything crunchy like a beetle. I was against Dave and I opened up the coconut, lifted the leaf and there was this big, jet black beetle crawling around. I started shaking. I shook more in the final and it was a mixture of adrenalin – because I knew if I lost it then we would go into the merger down – and fear. Actually, the beetle was not too bad. I picked it up as fast I could, bit off the head because it was poisonous and then took one bite and swallowed it. I did it as fast as I could because I knew that if I saw it crawling about in my hands then I would not be able to do it. I crunched it and swallowed it. Dave took ages to chew his." Dave pretended to pick morsels from his teeth as he swallowed his beetle. So far, neither side had defaulted.

Next were Susannah and Helen and their snack was worms and very lively worms too. When Susannah lifted her coconut, her worms were wriggling as if they were dancing the rumba, and Helen's too. "They were unbelievably lively," says Helen. "They could not keep still. I was laughing because I just couldn't pick them up – they kept running off." There had to be a cut when one of Susannah's worms made a bold dash for it and managed to escape, last seen bemoaning the rise of reality TV to his friends. More worms were brought, but these were no more static. Both Helen and Susannah struggled to keep their worms in their hands but eventually managed to get them down their throats without balking. "They tasted just like soil," Helen says.

Then it was Meeta and John, ready for his second course. They were faced with fat white worms. Meeta's act started immediately. "I f*cking knew it," she said when her dish was uncovered and looked suitably nauseated. From that point on, until the worm hit her stomach, she grimaced, groaned, mugged, swore, pouted and winced so much that South were in no doubt that she was the one they had to pick for the final head-to-head. It was a grandstand performance that her opponent across the table, Mr Showboat himself, John, would have appreciated, had he known it was not for real. For their part, North had decided on Jonny given his obvious distaste for the task ahead. So as it boiled down, it was Jonny vs Meeta to determine the make-up of the tribes at merger.

The final was, as Mark described, a "smorgasbord" of delicacies. Locusts, worms and the pièce de resistance, a live crab each. Jonny began shaking instantly. "I lost it. I could not stop myself shaking. I'd rather eat the fish eye and the bull's testicle because at least they weren't moving. I saw the dead locusts and thought 'They're not a problem.' I ate them first and then picked up the worms, dropped one of them because I was shaking but managed to eat them. Then I lifted up the coconut and saw the crab. It moved quickly and I had to catch it and swallow it whole. As I lifted it up it was up on its legs and I almost passed out. I remember Meeta trying to kill her crab using the back of the coconut. I picked mine up and dropped it, so I scooped it off the floor and put it in my mouth. John remembers it kicking its legs wildly, trying to fight its way out even when it was in my mouth. I just threw it back and crunched it as fast as I could. I swallowed it and we won. I was fine afterwards. Had it been a Reward Challenge then I'm not sure if I could have done it. But that changed the game completely."

Remarkably, no one was sick as a result of all this.

No one in North Island could blame Meeta for the effort she put in and, despite their obvious disappointment, they all believed she did the best she could. Meeta disagrees: she believes that, had she not wanted to get away from Panama as quickly as possible, then she could have won. She is not saying that she threw the game deliberately; simply, that she was unable to try her best. "I could have beaten him if I'd really gone for it. I chewed the locusts when they were dead and I could have just swallowed them. The crab I had a problem with. If I saw them on the island, I would have run. I could have done it, though. I wasted time chewing. Psychologically, I wasn't fully up for it, otherwise I think I could have won. I would have gone mad if I'd had to stay for the merger. I have pulled off some things in my life that I never thought I would and, had I wanted to do so, then I am certain I would have won this challenge. I was delighted that I was going home, absolutely ecstatic. The first thing that Helen said to me after the challenge was, 'You're going home, Meeta.' They were all happy for me. I wasn't unhappy we had lost at all." While she had been acting during her first "meal", her revulsion during the second course was for real. The crab truly repelled her.

South Island were ecstatic, however. They were going in to the merger on level terms and it was likely that each had achieved their ambition of making the jury. At 4-4 they would have to wait and see how the game would pan out but they would no longer be sitting ducks, waiting to be shot. Bridget was especially delighted because it was no secret she was the next in line to go if they had lost and it was her ultimate ambition to reach the merger. They returned to their island in great spirits, worried only by the news that the other tribe had discovered that Bridget had a vote against her and that could count at the first Tribal Council after merger on a split vote. In contrast, in North Island, only Meeta had a vote against her name and she was leaving. But the problem of who she would vote against was exercising her mind and that of her tribe. Someone claimed to have read in the rules that if a person failed to vote, i.e. left their voting slip blank, then that vote would count against them. But Ed Forsdick dismissed that belief, although Alastair claimed the rules were being changed as the game progressed. As Ed Forsdick pointed out, the rules also state that the executive producer has the right to overrule or change any aspect of the game and his decision is final. Forsdick also points out that for all their whingeing about past votes, if they had bothered to read the rules in any detail they would have realised that votes cast before merger were void afterwards anyway. Meeta also wanted to go, it was not as if she was withholding a vote for tactical reasons. Technically, by asking to leave, like Sarah before her, she was in breach of her contract. Therefore, she was forced to vote. While she accepted this, it caused Meeta some soul-searching on her last day on the island, day thirteen.

"The hardest thing the next day was deciding who to vote for. I didn't want to vote and we were told that if we didn't then the vote would be cast against you. Al approached Ed and asked if I could put in a blank vote and if it would count against me. Ed said I had to vote. I voted for Helen. We discussed it; she wasn't too happy. But I thought if they went into the merger then she would be the least likely to be voted off, because she wasn't the strongest. She might not agree. Dave I could never vote against because he's so lovely; Drew, I don't know, maybe she could have been voted off before Dave because she was a good competitor and really strong in the challenges."

Interestingly, that morning Alastair was up early and approached Meeta. He was obviously worried that her vote would go against him and wanted to persuade her to cast it elsewhere. Much as he is a good team man and a leader, Alastair was careful to look after himself at all times and preserve his own safety. "Al got up ten minutes after and came up to me and said, 'I feel really vulnerable,' meaning that if I voted for him he would have a back vote going into the merger. I fell for that I suppose. I always thought Alastair was cunning. We all swallowed his fuel cards lie. He is very convincing and confident. Basically, he's full of bullshit." But what made Alastair such an excellent leader of his tribe was the way he made people feel as if he wasn't leading them. He is very charismatic and flatters people, making them feel valued and involved and is never bossy or dictatorial, to the point where some members of North deny he was a leader and bristle when the question is put to them.

"I would disagree with the fact he was our leader," claims Drew. "We all came up with ideas and would discuss them. We all had a lot of good ideas and they were discussed and we came to decisions according to how everyone felt. There was never a case of Al saying such and such and we all do it. But on the other hand he is kind of a … no, I don't think he led the tribe actually but he is a strong character and he is somebody that we would look to and respect his decision. He made a lot of good decisions but then so did all of us. I know what you're saying and I can understand how it appears that way, but he was never domineering. I can see how it looked as if Al was in charge, and it might look that way on TV, and I know South Island saw Al as the leader of our tribe, and to a point he must have been some sort of leader but he never made all the decisions. Never." Helen echoes this view. Dave, however, accepts that Alastair was at the forefront of the decision-making in North. "He knew what he was doing. He's a big, bright lad and he knew more than me about some things. He never went ahead and did things. We would discuss it but a lot of the ideas came from him."

What was certain was that Alastair was right in one respect: South were going to target him. In the challenges he had shown himself to be a formidable competitor; he saw himself as the "Alpha Male"; he was vocal, bright and confident and he was devious and cunning. He had revealed his forces background to his tribe but he was still persisting with his story about being a fuel cards salesman.

That day Meeta spent preparing herself to go, dreaming

of home. There is a sense of disappointment about her, as if she can't believe how badly she coped with the conditions. "The weather was awful. At one point I wanted to see the psychologist because I thought I was losing it. I wanted to test my sanity. I started talking like Helen towards the end, which was a really bad sign. I was so pissed off I even started telling the cameramen to 'eff off' and leave me alone. Every time I thought of my brother, I wanted to go home, yet on the other hand a little voice was saying to me, 'Stay'. If I had a photo of him then I could have stayed, or if I could have spoken to him or my boyfriend. I don't know what was wrong with me, to be honest. I couldn't handle the fact that no one cared what happened to us. My legs were cut open and there was no one there to say it was all right. That was the worst thing."

No one has a bad word to say about Meeta, even though she had a few to say about them to camera during her stay. Dave says she's "smashing". "She has one of those smiles that lights up the whole place," he remembers, grinning himself at the memory. Both Helen and Drew recall her fondly. She is brassy, upfront, funny and vocal, with a sharp brain and wit to match. If she had conquered the conditions – the lack of food, the unending rain, the fact her tribe's beach was being eaten away, and the ever-present cameras – then she might well have been a decent player and gone far. But she did not have the staying power. She learnt a lot about herself, mainly that she is not quite as strong as she thinks she is. As someone who always valued her independence, she is now quite keen to settle down and have a family. She has overcome many problems in life that would have defeated lesser people, but she had no choice in doing that. It was for real. On *Survivor* she had a way out and she took it. It was much harder than she thought. To people who think she should have not gone on the programme in the first place, she says: "You don't know until you've been through it."

With Meeta gone there was a day of inactivity – day fourteen – while the contestants wondered about the forthcoming merger. To help them while away the hours they were given camcorders for the day and asked to make a film. The first thing that surprised both tribes was their own appearance in playback. No one could believe how much weight they had lost or how rough they looked. Getting over that original shock, they began to film their mini-documentaries. Their approach mirrored the character of each tribe: North took the opportunity to show how difficult their life had been, how the sea had eaten their beach and forced them to move camp. South, on the other hand, and John and Jonny in particular, used it to fool around and have fun at other people's expense, spoofing films like Taxi Driver and Top Gun.

One extract in particular was both revealing and hilarious. John and Jonny hog the camera, the former taking his chance to be Cecil B. De 16-mil; Susannah and Bridget make cameo appearances as the butt of the boys' gags.

> **John:** Jonny, what are your thoughts about the next couple of days then?
>
> **Jonny:** By the first Tribal Council of the merged tribe we will know who's won the whole *Survivor 2*. My prediction is that by Monday night, if that is the first Tribal Council, if North Island go ahead as the stronger, then Dave will definitely win … if North Island win. If South win then I don't know.
>
> **John:** Imagine how many Newcastle United season tickets he would buy with the money.
>
> **Jonny:** If we say he's a very nice man he might give us ten grand each.

John:	Dave, we think you're going to win, mate, we've always been with you.
Jonny:	I think Alastair is too ambitious for most of the other contestants.
John:	What makes you think Dave will do well, then?
Jonny:	He's just a likeable nice guy, inoffensive. Drew doesn't smile enough to win and Helen just wants to buy a house next to her Mum. I mean, how sad can you get for a 22-year-old. Go and buy some drugs like a normal 22-year-old and not buy the bloody house next door!
John:	Go and steal a car, for God's sake!
Jonny:	Go and commit some crime!
Bridget:	I hope my daughter doesn't see this; it'll give her ideas.
Jonny:	What 22-year-old wants to buy a house next door to her Mum? She might be lying; she might be a stripper in a lap-dancing bar … but I doubt it.
John:	Alastair will just buy some more growth hormone if he wins, more anabolic steroids.
John:	Bridget, what would you buy with a million?
Bridget:	I don't know. I'll carry on farming until it's all gone. What would you buy with a million pounds?
John:	You can't get away with it by asking me the same question. It doesn't work like that.
Jonny:	Put a lot of thought into it. What would you buy?
Bridget:	I'd go down the pub and order a round of drinks for everyone.
John:	Would you still drive your Peugeot 305?
Bridget:	Certainly, I love my little car. I don't know what I'd do. I'd put it in the bank.

John: Can I just give you a tip here on camera?
         Don't invest a million pounds in a current
         account.

Bridget: Why?

John: Just an investment tip.

Bridget: I need all the help I can get here.

John: It's all hypothetical anyway … until I get the
         million pounds.

Jonny: (To Bridget) If you give half a mill to me and
         half a mill to John then we'll invest it wisely
         for you.

John: The bank of "Jonny John". The bank of "The
         Gay Jonnies".

John: (To Jonny) How long do you think you will
         keep your job for when they see that bit of
         you doing the Village People on the karaoke?

Jonny: By the Monday following that episode I will
         be unemployed, homeless. Actually, I might
         get promoted! For equality and all that. I'll be
         the first gay Chief Constable! What would you
         do if you won a million pounds, John?

John: A million pounds? I'd give the lot to charity. I
         wouldn't touch it – dirty money.

Jonny: Would you get married?

John: I don't know. You'd have to ask my girlfriend.

Jonny: Because you're too short?

John: Unless I can get an operation to make me
         taller.

Jonny: Get your legs lengthened by a few inches.

John: A leg transplant from a normal sized man … A
         million quid? I'd marry Mary. I fancy a house
         by the Sydney Opera House. I tell you, the
         first thing I'd buy is some fly spray. I'd carry

on working though because it's a really good job. I think I'm doing really well at it. I just hope no judges watch this programme or I'll never work again.

Jonny: You'll get all the discrimination cases from all the gays wanting to join the forces.

John: All the gay policeman wanting to come out after Jonny made it in *Vogue*.

Jonny: Susannah, what's the first thing you would do with a million quid?

Susannah: A magnum of champagne. I'd bathe in it then drink it afterwards.

Jonny: I hope you'd wash before you do.

Susannah: I would definitely have a wash though it might mar the taste somewhat. I would buy a fantastic villa on the shores of Lake Como and have eight children and bake bread for the rest of my life.

Jonny: And deal coke?

Susannah: And deal coke …

Jonny: And what's the wildest place you've had sex.

Bridget: In a Jacuzzi …

John: In my bum …

Bridget: … I have to say it was with my ex-husband.

Jonny: This is so easy. Ask Bridget another question.

Bridget: Go on, ask me a really difficult question.

Jonny: If you could sleep with any member of the crew from *Survivor* who would it be?

John: Come on, Bridget, we know you've got a soft spot for some of them. Sausage? Isn't one of them called Sausage or Bacon or something? *(It's Sausage, a camera assistant whose real name is Neil Purcell.)*

Bridget: Duncan *(Gaudin, First Assistant Director)* is nice. Not Steve *(Docherty, Director)* he's too tall. Duncan's nearer my age.

Jonny I'm sure Duncan will like that.

John: Jonny, what kind of evening have you got planned when I come up to the Edinburgh Festival this summer?

Jonny: Well, as there are cameras watching … we will go for a nice meal, have a few beers, go and see Graham Norton and then have a couple of beers, then home and nice and early bed for an early rise for a run round.

John: And if you win the million tell me what the night will be?

Jonny: We will do the first three grams of coke off the dashboard of my brand-new Aston Martin.

John: That's you kicked off the show and your job. I feel I should point out as your lawyer at this stage to say nothing more on the subject.

Jonny: The two prostitutes can have a line each as well. Then we'd go and see some comedians and back for some roasted cheese made by Bridget … because she's won the million and I've married her. What would you like to do when you come up to Edinburgh, John?

John: With or without the million?

Jonny: Without the million first.

John: Pick me up at the station in your car and your warrant card. You can put the blue light on top and we can arrest a few people for a laugh. I'll bring my wig and gown and we can pretend

it's a 24-hour court. Then we can go out and
see a couple of comedy shows at the festival,
a few beers, reminisce over old times and
watch the video of when I win the million
again. Then I'll be off to the Caribbean leaving
you in squalor.

Jonny: What about you, Susannah, when you come
up and visit?

Susannah: What, are you going to treat me too?

Jonny: Bridget, what are you going to do when you
come and visit us?

Bridget: You're going to take me around and show me
the sights.

John: I don't think you'll like it.

Bridget: Why's that?

John: It's full of Scots people.

Bridget: I get on all right with Scots people, Irish
people and the Welsh.

Jonny: Susannah, what are you going to treat us to
down in London?

Susannah: The most enormous thick chocolate mousse
you could ever imagine … and that's it.

John: It's hardly worth the train fare is it?

Jonny: I think I'll come and visit you instead, John.
What are you going to treat us to in London?

John: I don't live in London, but if I did …

Jonny: Well, London, England, it's all the same to us
Jocks.

John: I'd take you down to the cathedral in
Winchester.

They are told they have one more minute to film.

Jonny:	Closing credits.
John:	Thank you very much to the crew.
Bridget:	Who aren't here.
John:	Thank you very much for being given the opportunity out of the 7500 who have applied to come out to this beautiful place and (he looks up at the boom mikes) have two big furry things dangled over my head.
Jonny:	That happens to you every night …

As is evident, morale in South Island was high. They had salvaged what seemed to be a dire position and made it through to the merger without disadvantage, discounting the votes that had been cast against them. This was the last time both tribes would have for such levity before the situation became more tense and a combination of the weather, the merger and the new environment to which they soon moved sapped everyone's spirits and destroyed their sense of humour. Over the next few days, jokes were scarce.

Week 3

Mutiny!

The weather had grown increasingly appalling throughout the first two weeks of *Survivor*, but it reached its crescendo on day fifteen, the point when South and North ceased to exist and became one tribe. Their old islands were to be left behind and a new home was found. When the programme makers had performed a recce, Isla Popa had looked like paradise on earth; the weather was better, sandy beaches, fish in abundance and a fresh water source. These details were woven into the script Mark Nicholas used when he addressed the tribes at the merger ceremony. Unfortunately, although the island had been checked again just 36 hours before merger and still looked fine, some insistent rain had detracted from the appearance of Isla Popa somewhat by the time of merger, as the contestants would discover to their displeasure.

At 6am the remaining eight made their way to Salt Creek. They walked through an Indian village and then had to undergo a two-hour trek to a waterfall at the island's centre. Throughout the whole ordeal the rain fell in torrents, soaking everyone. As they made their way deeper into the jungle, the rain became more persistent and it became muddier and muddier. Eventually they came to a stop at the waterfall and were ordered to remove their tribal colours. Then as they stood shivering in the rain, Mark, wrapped snugly in his raincoat and hat, told them about the island that would become their new home. Dripping wet, cold and miserable as they were, it sounded idyllic. Then they were instructed to think of a new name for their new tribe and that he would see them the next day at the Reward Challenge. He also informed them that waiting at their new home was an island-warming treat in the shape of a barbecue, three chickens, hamburgers, a basket of fruit and six bottles of red wine. Things were looking up – or so they thought.

The reality was different: pleasant as the burgers and booze were, they were insignificant when compared to the state of the island. Mark's description had elevated everybody's expectations but they were faced with what Helen bluntly but perhaps accurately described as a "sh*thole". "Desert island, my arse," as Dave said in best Jim Royle fashion. The area that had been designated for them to build their shelter was like a bog; it was also infested with fire ants that delivered a stinging nip; if you walked into the sea you sank to your knees in black silt. The weather was no different; the rain was still unrelenting. It would be an understatement to say that the eight remaining Survivors were not amused, and the view was unanimous, as some of these comments reveal.

"We were sinking in the mud. But it was when the fire ants attacked me that I got annoyed." (Alastair); "We got there and it had been pissing with rain. Everywhere was sodden and we all thought, 'What? We have to build a camp here? It's horrible.' There were a few frayed tempers – mainly mine." (Bridget); "We started building the shelter and then all of a sudden we started getting bitten by these bloody ants. The pain was terrible. It was like two wasps mugging you. Jesus Christ! Everyone was doing a war dance. Then there were poisonous red frogs and we thought, 'What sort of place have we come to?' It was absolutely terrible. It stank." (Dave); "We were told we were going to a kinder environment with more food; there would be pineapples and loads of other fruit, blah blah blah. Of course, it just rained and rained and rained and we were absolutely soaked through and no dry kit. The area we were allocated to set up our camp was completely infested with ants and we were ankle-deep in mud. The first few days were horrendous." (Drew); "They promised all these brilliant things about where we were going, and we got there and it were like Glastonbury. We wanted to go back to South Island. As soon as the rain stopped it was brilliant, but we felt really let down." (Helen); "The weather was horrendous. We were told to wear boots at all times and half of us couldn't put on our boots because we had cuts and sores and blisters. It was totally impractical given how wet it was." (Jonny); "There were lots of different factors: the weather was atrocious; we had been told to camp in one place and it was not feasible because the mud was so deep and there were ants everywhere and the mosquitoes were ridiculous. Plus there was no way it would have dried out. The island had very few natural resources; there were few palm trees and very few coconuts, which had become a staple of our diet. We could not build an adequate shelter to keep the rain out. We were also not allowed to go beyond certain boundaries, which was a big thing from my point of view, searching for food. It was because there were several poisonous snakes on that part of the island. Our area was cleared of them." (Susannah); "It was never that bad." (John).

John was in the minority, however, and he agreed with the view that they should seek another place to pitch camp rather than the one recommended to them. The men went searching for a better place and eventually came across a spot on a peninsula, on top of a small hill. It was less muddy and the ants less rampant but there was danger in traversing its slopes because of the mud. All the indecision about whether to stay or go began to get on Bridget's nerves. The day had been tense and she was getting fed up with people's moaning. In her opinion, there were too many chiefs and very few Indians. "Four had become eight and I'd mainly been Mum on one island and the two girls from North Island started doing the cooking. I didn't like it. There's a few heated bits of me saying my piece to camera when my father will watch it and turn around and say, 'Yes, that's my Bridget.' Everyone was moaning about their feet hurting. Well, the North Island girls were moaning about that and I just turned around and said, 'All our f**king feet are hurting. Get on with it.' When they were talking about moving sites to a better place, I said, 'For God's sake make up your mind.' The day was getting shorter and we were running out of light."

Susannah shared her frustration at the whining and moaning that Helen and Drew were indulging in. "My tolerance level for Helen and Drew was very low at the beginning because they had blisters, so they couldn't do any physical work. I was like, 'Everyone has blisters. Everyone is hurting in some way and you just have to get on with it.' I was crotchety towards them because at that time I saw them as a pathetic waste of space."

The men decided to move eventually and John told everyone Alastair would inform them where, which upset Alastair because it immediately pushed him to the forefront. But, to be honest, there are few other places for Alastair to be. There was then a race against the clock to get the new shelter erected before the light closed in. People were keen to get their hands on the burgers and the wine. It had been such a lousy day that getting drunk seemed the best way to round it off. Unfortunately, while everyone enjoyed the burgers, they made quite a few people sick or gave them the runs. Their shrunken stomachs, used to so little, simply failed to cope with rich food, no matter how delicious. Of course, it had nothing to do with copious quantities of red wine. That night, they all sat inside their shelter in their waterproofs, getting wetter and wetter, but insulated by the booze, telling rude jokes. Conditions were so bad that politicking was out of the question; simply getting hold of the red wine and keeping up their spirits was the summit of everyone's ambition.

They swapped stories about Sarah, Tayfun, Meeta and Lee. It was like a pub, with several conversations going on at once, though six bottles of red wine might last longer than 45 minutes in a pub. Bridget, for the first time, encountered Helen's propensity for colourful language. "Does your mother know you swear so much?" she asked. "It was her that f**king learnt me," came the reply. This continued into the night until they decided to get some rest.

But rest was impossible; the rain did not cease and the shelter would not have passed any inspection under the Trade Descriptions Act, despite having every available palm frond piled upon it. They had piled everything they could on the top. There was no shortage of initiative being used but the rain still cascaded in. Bridget eventually decided to sleep outside on the basis that it was as wet in the rain as it was in the shelter. The floor was so wet that Drew simply refused to lie down and spent the whole night standing up. As John recalls, the conditions were worsening rather than improving. "The first night was so miserable. I lay beside this palm tree and the rain was pouring down. When I woke up I was moving – the ground was shifting beneath me, it was so wet." The next morning he got up and literally wrung out his jumper.

It was the worst night so far and the longest. No one slept. By the next morning everyone was tired, hung over and thoroughly fed up. Helen and Drew refused to come out of the shelter. Despite the efforts of the crew to ask them to do something, anything, they could film, the contestants would not co-operate. Dark murmurs of mutiny began to spread. People's feet were beginning to rot because of the wet conditions. The crew were also finding it difficult to move around because of the mud – it was more like Isla Somme than Isla Popa. Alastair felt that, if they were being asked to survive, then their main priority would be staying dry, not wasting pointless energy getting wet just so the cameras could have something to film. "We thought it was insensitive to ask us to get into soaking wet canoes to go to their challenges, get wet and come back. A lot of anger was vented on the production company. We just thought, 'Sorry, just to fit in with your schedule we are going to be soaking and freezing all night. That's not very considerate.' " He even thought getting wet performing the games was too much. "We were saying that if we were surviving we wouldn't be doing this. We would be seeking shelter." An odd argument: as if the games were just an adjunct to their survival rather than an integral part of it.

For Helen, it was a matter of "respect". "We went to sleep that first night and the mud was really deep and I thought, 'I don't want to be here.' It lowered our morale and we just sat in the tent not able to do anything. People said, 'It's for a million pounds' and yes, it is for a million pounds and there's playing the game, which we were doing, but there's no reason to do it under those conditions."

One has to ask what they were expecting: Butlins? Yes, the conditions were awful; yes, the island failed to live up to the hyperbole; yes, the suggested site for the first camp was inadequate and yes, surviving was extremely difficult. But there was a million pounds at stake here and no one said it was going to be easy. A simple complaint that something needed to be done because people's feet, like Dave and John who had been cut, were rotting would have been sufficient. Instead some of the Survivors, like Drew and Helen, took whinging to a new level. What ever happened to bearing problems stoically? Perhaps this lot had become too pampered. There is also a sneaking suspicion that a true Survivor would not have joined in with the "woe is us" chorus; someone like Andy from the last series of *Survivor* would have welcomed the awful conditions on the basis that the tougher it gets, the fewer people will be able to stand it. People will start asking to go and those willing to stick it out can then come into their own. This was a thought that crossed Jonny's mind, who together with John, is one of the few that dismissed the "mutiny" as discontented rumbling and no more.

"I wasn't going to mutiny," says Jonny. "As far as I was concerned, people were just gutted. People weren't too bothered about the prospect of being voted off but I was thinking that we had two weeks down, there was only another 23 days to go and I knew I could sit in that shelter for three weeks if I knew a million was at the end of it. I wasn't happy with it but in my head I knew I could put up with it. It's a million pounds. I've worked for the last ten years and got nowhere near earning that so I think I could put with hardship for another 23 days, however miserable."

The production team, however, could not ignore the fact that, as a result of the extraordinary weather conditions, people were running a severe risk of injury and infection. The mud made the peninsula slopes so slippery that it seemed only a matter of time until someone was seriously injured, either crew or contestant. Dave had already taken a spectacular tumble walking down the slope. The state of people's feet was a worry. To try to ease the malcontents among the contestants, Ed Forsdick ventured out to the island seeking to broker peace, and spoke to each in turn, hearing their grievances. When it was Bridget's turn, he looked around at the mud and grime and asked, "You'll be used to this won't you?" John told him that his worries were purely from a health and safety aspect. After hearing all the evidence, he decided something had to be done before injury struck or trench foot set in. Later that day, after the reward challenge, Mark arrived on the island to collect Drew and Susannah's dirty clothing to be laundered, and gave them a tarpaulin that would at least keep the rain from within the shelter. A walkway was also constructed up and down the peninsula to allow crew and contestants to make their way without fear of falling. The new tarpaulin made all the difference to the shelter, keeping the rain out and all the contents dry – a novelty for all the contestants, who were used to living in wet clothes. It also meant they had a chance of sleep that evening. Ironically, this presentation coincided with an improvement in the weather.

The overall consequence of this episode, however, was to bring the new tribe – "Columbus", named after the man who "discovered" the islands – together. There was definitely an element of "them and us" because it was clear that people would still vote according to tribal allegiances but the overall atmosphere was harmonious. As Susannah points out, "We couldn't sleep; we couldn't eat because we couldn't start a fire; we couldn't get dry and we couldn't wash ourselves. The thought of participating in challenges was a million miles away. It was basic survival. No one was thinking of a million pounds because we were concentrating on eating and sleeping." People accepted that there was no point in scheming until the first Tribal Council decided which tribe would be at a numerical disadvantage. Then the game playing could start. Until then,

North were set on voting off John, should they be given the chance, while South's target was Alastair.

The one spoke in all this was Bridget, who was becoming increasingly fractious about the contribution of some tribe members. The change in circumstances appeared to have disoriented her. On South Island, she had a place, a role, which she was happy to fulfil. In Columbus her role was not so clear and her patience was pushed to breaking point. It was noticed by Susannah, Jonny and John and they hoped to take the opportunity to tell her to watch her step. Their minds were taken off it by the breath-holding Reward Challenge, the first since merger, which gave everyone the chance to focus their minds on something other than the weather conditions. This game was similar to that in series 1; two heats of four contestants holding onto a log underwater for as long as possible. The winners would then take place in a final where they would have to haul in a small log using a rope while sitting underwater. It was a dead heat between Drew and Susannah, who it seemed were vying for the post of "Alpha Female". Their reward was the luxury item they chose before the game started – for Drew a photo of her boyfriend, Robin, for Susannah *The Complete Works of Shakespeare* – and a choice each of someone else's luxury item. They chose Dave's football and Helen's hammock, turning down Bridget's boules, Jonny's inflatable armchair, John's picture of his girlfriend and Alastair's Frisbee. Even better was the additional reward of having their clothes collected and laundered, returned to them the next day clean and fresh. The rest, in their sodden, muddy clothing, looked on in envy. But at the end of day sixteen, a long one for everyone, they all went to bed that night drier and much, much happier.

The next day they awoke, having slept, fully expecting the first and crucial Immunity Challenge since merger. Picking up the Treemail, they were puzzled however, because it seemed as if they would be going straight to a vote, with no challenge. Alastair was particularly worried, because it meant this could be his last day on the island. He was getting paranoid because he had noticed the gender split within the tribe, with the women working together and the men doing likewise. He feared some element of alliance building could develop as a consequence. In reality, everyone was thrown by the Treemail and the fact that it seemed they would be voting someone off that evening. Dave even suggested that the whole game might be cut short because of the appalling weather.

The Geordie could not make up his mind who to vote off, Bridget or John. With the lack of an Immunity Challenge and the prospect of a straight vote, the smart money was on Bridget because North had learned she had a vote against her already, while they did not, apart from Helen. There were other reasons. "The first night we were here on Isla Popa," Dave told the camera, "it was horrendous conditions and everybody was really mucking in a lot and Bridget seemed to lose her temper a bit. Everyone was shocked by the conditions we were confronted with and she lost it a bit. She has been ratty here and maybe that's because she had a bad day. I don't know." Asked who he thought the strongest person in the whole tribe was, he answered emphatically, "It's Drew. I think she has been the secret weapon for us from the start. I think that she is a secret weapon and I think she could be the opposition if I get to the final."

It was true that Drew was coming further out of her self and becoming more confident the longer the game progressed. This was not always betrayed on camera where she was reticent and wary, reluctant to divulge what she was thinking. But around the camp she was more outgoing and friendly. South Island were slowly adapting their opinion of her, having mercilessly poked fun at her in private for looking so miserable. All, that is, except for Bridget, with whom Drew did not get on. Despite emerging from her shell, Drew did not share Dave's view that she was a candidate to win. "I haven't got any whoopee-do strategies. If I am completely honest, I don't see myself winning the million pounds. I haven't come out here for just the money. I have come to see how far I am capable of pushing myself. If I was to win I'd be the most surprised person in the world but at the moment I don't have any plans for hiding the rice or pissing people off or trying to get in with other people. I find it hard to be someone I'm not. I am aware that I could be bitchy but you are not guaranteed to win the million even if you are bitchy and you have to live with that and that fact that millions of people have seen you like this. I wouldn't want my friends or family or work seeing me like that." This was a view other survivors had shared; they had watched last year as the contestants tore each other to shreds and vowed not to come across as such appalling people. Apart from Susannah that is, whose *Complete Works of Shakespeare* had several messages from her family who knew she was going on the programme. From her husband Barney, was the message, "Shaft everyone – and prepare to be shafted!" But even she had been affected by guilt after turning tail on Lee.

South Island had seen close up how tight Helen, Drew and Alastair were. They were desperately trying to discover which member had a vote against them, and Jonny's gut feeling was telling him it was Drew or Alastair. His gut was wrong. Within an hour of being on the island, Alastair had informed them that North would be voting for Bridget and Jonny's dislike and distrust of Alastair fermented further. John's reason for not liking Alastair was slightly different: "I sleep beside him and every time he moves the whole shelter buckles in half," he told the camera. He had told everyone he was in the Marines for two reasons: Alastair had approached him directly and asked him and he decided to be honest; secondly, he did not want to misrepresent himself. He reaffirmed his loyalty to the alliance he had built with Jonny and Susannah, and joined with Jonny in stating that the nicest of the other bunch was Dave. Tellingly, he gave one insight that would play a big part in Susannah's chances of winning. "It has been interesting to hear so many regional accents under one roof. I would be very surprised if the English-speaking world can understand what we are saying. Alastair, Jonny and myself are the token Celts, Dave the Geordie, Helen with the strongest Northern accent I think I have ever heard. I think Susannah feels a bit out of place with her Home Counties accent."

This problem for Susannah would become more apparent as the days passed. Dave, for one, could not get over the way she spoke. "Susannah is the poshest woman I've ever met – she makes the Queen sound like a slag. I've never known a woman speak so proper. She pronounces everything so well and I thought, 'God, she's oozing with money this lass.' " In many people's minds, posh voice equalled money and nothing would shake it short of Susannah producing a bank statement from her back pocket. There was another incident in the shelter that many of the contestants remember, which fed the impression that Susannah was rather more affluent than she made out.

"One night in the shelter we started talking about cars and asking what people had," Dave adds. "I told them I had a P-reg Hyundai, Jonny had a battered Fiesta and there was no word from Susannah. I asked her and she said, 'Oh, just a rusty old bike.' Then I asked her about her husband and she said, 'Barney' – I mean Barney, that's what you call a dog, man – 'has got a BMW convertible.' I'm not into cars and Al asked what model it was and we worked out it was about £50,000 worth and I thought, 'Aye, aye, this woman's got money.' Everywhere we talked about regarding foreign countries, because I've been to a few places with the Navy, she'd been to all of them. Every place I mentioned, her and Barney had been there. She'd only been married for four years! I thought she'd got money. She never admitted it but there's something about her she's never said. She's a well-educated lass, nice personality. But she's so posh. I've never heard anyone talk like her."

In reality, she lives in a small terraced house in Wimbledon that is only half-decorated because she and Barney ran out of money halfway through. She can accept this sort of view from Dave, though she understandably gets angry about Alastair's criticism that "she pleads poverty" although she was born with a silver spoon in her mouth when he walked into a hugely-paid job with the family firm after leaving the armed forces. But Alastair happens to speak with a broad Scottish accent.

"People saw me as posh and there was very little I could do to dispel that view. I just tried to get on with Dave as best I could. I tried to find common ground. Obviously, Dave will have judgements about me and, if someone wants to believe something, then there's nothing I could do to persuade them otherwise. I decided just to be myself. It pissed me off that people thought I was born with a silver spoon in my mouth. There's Alastair who works for a family firm and is on £150,000 a year or something. Also, Bridget owns an amazing amount of land and admitted as much. There's Drew, who I'm sure did not have that different an upbringing from me. My parents live in a three-bedroom house on a main A-road going into Reading. Not a bloody mansion. This whole idea was misinformed. The regional accents mask this idea of class and wealth. Because I speak with a Home Counties accent and I speak properly because I've done lots of drama, the perception is different. John's a barrister with a nice flat. What can I do? Apart from saying to Dave, 'When we get back I'll show you around my

house and around my parents' house. Here's my bank balance.'
North Island had formed an opinion of me without knowing me
and they were unable to shed it. John had a shared military
background with Alastair; Jonny had the whole public service
thing with Drew and Dave and I felt that they had made their
minds up about me and that was not going to change. All I
could do was be myself and make them see I wasn't trying to
be anything I wasn't, that I worked hard and I was a nice girl."

She did herself few favours with the Shakespeare, however,
and there are times when perhaps she should have moderated
the way she communicated, where she was guilty of trying
too hard. She was playing the game to win, as she
readily admits, so the accusation that she was ambitious is correct
and should not be seen as a pejorative. But more pervasive
among North Island was the view that she was "condescending"
and "false" in the way she interacted. All of North Island prided
themselves on their down-to-earth, a spade's-a-spade attitude
and Susannah's manner grated a bit. Unfortunately, there was
little Susannah could do about her voice, unless she was to
employ her drama background and enact a reversal of *My Fair
Lady*, burying her cut-glass accent beneath a broad cockney
twang. But it is interesting that the way she spoke made people
think she was devious and manipulative. Perhaps it had more to
do with the fact that she is confident, ambitious and strong and
these are attributes accepted in a man and seen as
undesirable in a woman.

Despite the class conflict that was bubbling under the
surface, and the fact she had let a chicken escape that day
before Bridget and Drew recovered it, Susannah was safe at the
evening's Tribal Council. As, indeed, was everyone else. Having
packed their rucksacks, they were surprised to learn that no one
would be going home. Instead, they were delighted to hear
from Mark Nicholas that each person voted off would be going

on the jury. They would form a jury of six, augmented by a seventh member – the Great British public – who would get the chance to vote by telephone during the final show. The other important news they were given concerned previous votes. All votes against a person's name before the merger were declared null and void. The slate was wiped clean. If there was a tied vote then the two people involved would have to make a speech stating their case to stay on the island, then there would be another vote. This caused consternation among some, Alastair in particular, because it obliterated their strategy to vote off Bridget. He was not happy, accusing the programme-makers of changing the rules as they went along, but he had to accept it. Deliberately, the contestants were not told what would happen if, when they next came to Tribal Council, a split vote was still recorded after the speeches had been made. They would have to wait and see.

Arriving back at camp, there was a lot for them to take in. The Night Producer expressed surprise that all eight had returned. Even the crew were kept unaware of what was going on for fear that the information might filter its way through to the contestants. John joked, "We voted Ed off." Humour aside, all the contestants knew that the next Immunity Challenge was the one upon which the whole game hinged as long as people stuck to their first tribal alliances. John and Alastair were the targets again and it was vital that they should try to win immunity. Then it would be a case of waiting to see how a split vote would be reconciled at the next Tribal Council.

The interactive element gave the game another dimension. Of course, given that six members of Columbus would form the jury, how people were perceived by their tribe mates was important, as they would be the major factor in deciding who would win. But knowing the viewers at home may be given the casting vote meant that people would have to consider the way they came across on camera. Their public image was a concern. With this to cogitate on, a cagey bonhomie settled on the tribe. Not only would outright bitchiness or lowdown sneaky behaviour cost them dearly if witnessed by other contestants, if they were to issue forth their frustrations on camera and denounce someone strongly, it might not play well with people in their sitting-rooms. The game would therefore favour someone with the ability to befriend as many people as possible, to save their spite and bile for private moments, away from the cameras, and to come across as a worthy winner to the viewers at home by excelling in the challenges. That person would also have to be very careful about whom they took into the final two with them; the ideal scenario would be going up against the most unpopular person on the island. That would mean Dave's chances looked poor, having claimed the unofficial title of "Most Popular Survivor". There was a time under Kevin Keegan's stewardship when, because of their buccaneering style of football, Dave's beloved Newcastle United were everyone's second favourite club behind the one they supported. Dave was the same; if they were not to win themselves, almost everyone, including those who had been ejected prior to merger, said they wanted Dave to win. Therefore, his overall chances of winning were nil – a bit like Keegan's Newcastle.

'Two Jocks and One Paddy Standing on a Log'

Day eighteen dawned and with it a row. Unsurprisingly, it involved Bridget and Drew who had been circling each other warily since merger. The subject of the row was the cockerel and how it should be slaughtered. Bridget, a veteran of many kills, was the accepted expert on such matters and was calmly about to demonstrate to Alastair how a good, clean kill should be approached. Drew was concerned about the feelings of the other chickens, in the cage while their companion was killed in front of them. Drew is an animal lover; so is Bridget, but they come from separate points on the spectrum. Living with death every day, and a supporter of fox-hunting, Bridget had no problem with killing the bird in front of the others. Drew, however, thought it would distress the others. Bridget was not having it, labelling Drew's view silly. "But, if you want it killed over there, then we will kill it over there," she added abruptly and walked off in what could best be described as a huff. Bridget might know more about killing and slaughtering animals but she was in danger of lording it over the others. The tension was obvious.

Another row flared later concerning the chicken. Drew believed that no part of the chicken should be spared and that they should even eat the head. Bridget wanted nothing to do with this suggestion and made her distaste clear. There then followed an interminable debate about the merits and demerits of eating chicken heads, with Bridget firmly an anti and Drew a pro. Bridget's inability to control her frustration and bite her tongue when those who knew less than her proffered an opinion was causing unease throughout the tribe, and was worrying John, Jonny and Susannah. They felt that Bridget was marking herself down to be voted off next and were keen to urge her to cool it. It is part of Bridget's character, however, as she readily admits. "I lost the plot a little bit with Drew. It wasn't much. It was all over the chicken and a part of its neck. I said, 'You don't want to eat that' and she said we should, we should eat everything. She wanted to eat the head and I don't care who you are, you don't eat that bit of the chicken. The next day, I made my apologies and that was accepted. I am quite difficult with change; for a couple of days it tends to get to me then I settle down. That's how it went."

Susannah was the one chosen to have a word with Bridget

in private. She deduced that Bridget's attitude to Drew and Helen had hardened since learning the public would have a say in the results. "It was a really trying time because people starting showing their real colours at that point. Bridget was a different person on that second island. She started not to make an effort with other people. If she had a problem with someone, she would tell them, and she really started to pick fights with Drew. I told Bridget to calm it down. She was winding Drew up massively and she was pissing off other members of North Island so I told her that for her own preservation, she needed to get on with people. She said to me, 'It is really important that you and I look strong on camera and show the girls up to look completely crap, because the public need to see that we are a lot better than them.' She had not worked out that she would not even get to that point if she was antagonising the girls that much. She decided she needed to look good on camera and used telling Drew off in order to achieve that. She really had not thought everything through. I told her she'd come across so badly and that she would piss off the others and be voted off."

The former South Islanders' reaction seemed a trifle excessive. Bridget and Drew did not get on but so what? Personality clashes were always going to happen with people living in such close proximity under such trying conditions. There is a sense here, not for the first time, that South were using Bridget like some sort of puppet, controlling her behaviour. All she seemed to be guilty of was being herself; she is not the most patient of people, but then *Survivor* does not always reward patience. Bridget duly apologised but it cut no ice with Drew. "Bridget is bossy and a different person to the sort I get on with. I find her false and find it hard to warm to her. But she's not malicious." Once again, her pro-foxhunting views and right-wing politics did not sit easily with more politically correct members of the tribe. Funnily enough, Dave, who strongly disagrees with the idea of female firefighters, a cause for which Drew is a zealous battler – she is one of only four in the whole of Oxfordshire – escaped such censure. But then his natural charm and easy wit mean Dave could probably get away with calling all Sunderland supporters sub-human. And probably does.

Everybody was looking forward to eating the chicken because for three days they had hardly eaten and everyone was feeling sapped of energy and strength. The weather had gone from the ridiculous to the sublime; from pouring rain to baking sun, the temperature rising well into the nineties Fahrenheit. After more than a fortnight of covering every inch of their bodies to keep dry and warm, people were now trying to prevent themselves from burning or getting heat stroke. No one was complaining though. The persistent rain had affected the spirits of everyone, contestants and crew alike. The sun improved everyone's mood.

That afternoon's Reward Challenge was "Broken Spears", which was won by Drew "by sheer luck" she admits. It was not a physically taxing game. Her prizes were a sleeping bag, a knife and fork and a mess kit. It would prove useful that evening for the great chicken feast, with all the usual bone sucking and fat slurping. The two factions were just beginning to get the measure of each other, though Alastair seemed to have been spreading misinformation among the former members of South Island. Jonny and Susannah spoke that evening about how Alastair had informed him that they might not be voting as a four, but instead have two voting for the strongest person, John, and the other two voting for the person they liked least. "That'll be me then," added Bridget, who had joined them. But, as Jonny, pointed out, it made no sense because if they stuck to voting as a block then the others would lose a member. Both took the opportunity to ask Bridget to mind her tongue in front of Helen and Drew. "I feel threatened by Drew in every single way," Bridget admitted. Her mood was not helped when Susannah said she had overheard Drew moaning to Helen about that morning's disagreement. Bridget pointed out, rightly, that she had nothing to apologise for. "The problem is that there are three mothers up there but only one of us actually is," she added sagely. On South Island, the fire had been hers; here, she had rivals. Jonny, ever the diplomat, finally quelled Bridget's concerns with an arm around her shoulder. Straight afterwards, Susannah admitted that, basically, they had been telling her off. The mother was being mothered. Bridget focused her dislike of Drew on trying to get farther than her, thus winning the battle of the headlines in the *Oxford Mail*: "Farmer beats Firefighter" is how she envisioned it reading.

Tensions were also voiced about space in the tent, the view being that Alastair and Helen and Drew took up far too much and refused to sleep top and tail. That wasn't a problem the next evening, because almost half the members of the tribe weren't there: they were standing on a log.

For many people, the log stand was the highlight of the first series of *Survivor*. Andy Fairfield, a 40-year-old helicopter pilot from Oxfordshire, won the respect and admiration of millions of viewers when he managed to stand on a log nine inches in diameter for 23 long, ankle-aching hours in blazing heat, pitch darkness and pouring rain, while Richard Owen, a psychiatrist, tried every mind game in the book to force him off. Realising that Andy could not and would not be broken and mindful of his swollen feet, Richard finally gave in and Andy won. That victory turned him into many people's favourite and the feat became a major talking point. Who would have thought that standing on a log for a day would make such compelling viewing?

Among those watching this feat at home was Jonny Gibb, a 31-year-old detective from Edinburgh. It was the first episode he had seen of *Survivor* and he was hooked. When he heard that a second series was planned, he applied, along with his girlfriend Ruth. Both reached the first interview stage – though they did not tell Planet 24 of their relationship – but only Jonny was chosen. If it had not been for Andy's amazing endurance he might not have been in Bocas. But from the moment he was selected he earmarked the log stand as "his" challenge: the one he would win.

His incentive, other than beating Andy's record, was his nephew Daniel. "I thought my nephew would be really proud watching me do it. Before I left, I told him I was going to the jungle and he asked if I had a tent. I said I did and he asked if I watched *Survivor*. 'Just do what they did,' he said, 'it's easy.' While I was away he asked my sister if she thought I had met the *Survivor* people yet, thinking that *Survivor* goes on constantly around the world. I saw the log stand last year and thought it was really impressive, that focus, willpower and determination. I wanted to test myself. I wanted to sit beside my nephew Daniel and watch me win it. My sister is a single parent and I have tried to be a role model for him, a father figure I suppose. I take him swimming, or to the pictures. I knew John was fitter and faster than I was; I knew Alastair was stronger than I was; I knew Susannah was more intelligent than I was; but this challenge was one I could do. When I give something my full determination there is no one who can beat me. No one. I thought this was the one. No matter what, I was not coming off that log, unless I collapsed."

Everyone was waiting for the vital Immunity Challenge and

as soon as they read the Treemail they guessed what it was going to be.

Mark Nicholas
requests the pleasure of your company
for the
1st Columbus Immunity Challenge
at Shark Restaurant

Date: Today
Dress: Informal
RSVP not required

"Who's Mark Nicholas?" John joked. Jonny announced that this would be his challenge; Alastair spoke of his hope of lasting as long as possible, John also. They wanted to beat Andy's record and they were determined to do it. Listening in, many of the female members were intimidated by such talk; they knew they would not be able to compete. All the focus was on the afternoon from then on, with time only for Dave to tell the camera that he was worried that Alastair had a secret plan and for Susannah to express astonishment at how much Helen and Drew relied on him. Before leaving she and Jonny decided it was Alastair for whom they would vote: "Let's f*ck him," they said defiantly. Then it was time to slap on the sunscreen and leave for the log.

The log was set up 20 metres out to sea from a small fishermen's staging post, its dimensions nine inches in diameter, the same as last year's challenge. Sitting at a table laid in waiting was Mark, with the promise that those who fell or jumped in would have the chance of a cold beer and shark steak meal. Before the eight swam out to take their positions on the log, Jonny and John made a pact to ensure they were next to each other in order to give each other full support for the ordeal ahead. As they climbed on at 2.30pm they all realised something that last year's contestants also learned quickly: that with eight people on board, the log wobbles a great deal. Finding your balance was not easy and there was a real prospect of falling in. Jonny was shocked. "For the first ten minutes I was amazed how shaky it was. I panicked, thinking that I might come off straight away and this was the one I wanted to win. I was telling people not to move because I thought I might go in." It dawned on a few that the game was about balance and not just mind-control, at least initially.

Dave started singing, prompting John to warn him that if he carried on then he would have to jump in. He need not have worried because Dave, in the process of telling Alastair a joke, lost control after 30 minutes and was the first to go, a cry of "Oh shit" echoing around the creek as he plunged backwards. He was surprised he did so badly. "I thought I'd be good at it as well because in the pub I never sit down, I always stand up. This is my game. I thought, 'I'm going to beat that cocky idiot's record from last year,' because that bloke Andy was full of himself, wasn't he? I thought 24 hours, no bother. But it was so wobbly and the first half hour was all about getting your balance, because as soon as somebody moved, that was it. We started cracking jokes. I turned to Alastair to crack one and I went back to deliver the punchline, but I turned too quick and my concentration went. I just thought, 'Oh no.' I knew I was going and I thought, 'Please God, stick us back on it, eh?' Then I said, 'Oh shit!' "

The next person to feel uncomfortable was Drew who suffers from curvature of the spine. Elsewhere, the chatter started, between John, Jonny and Susannah, though Jonny would break off to scold anyone for any sudden movements. John lamented not having seen *Lord of the Rings* before leaving England. It would have made for good practice, being a film that makes standing on a log for a day seem interesting in comparison. Alastair warned Susannah he would bore her off, a threat she took seriously having already spent four days with him. Drew, after just over an hour, started to get pains in her back and decided to avoid causing herself any lasting damage by getting off. With two gone, the remaining six found it much easier to balance. Only two and a half hours in the singing started. Already it looked like being a long night for everyone.

Verbal noughts and crosses were followed by verbal chess, followed by Shakespeare. Jonny cracked a joke, John almost fell in laughing and Helen began fantasising once again about her chocolate fudge cake. When Mark announced the three hour mark they all broke out into a Mexican wave. Susannah expressed a worry about getting nappy rash through wearing wet knickers while Helen looked forward to her tea. Then it got worse; less than four hours in and they were already reminiscing about children's TV programmes. For someone who has such distaste for idle chit-chat, John was surprisingly good at it. Someone told him he looked small stood between Alastair and Jonny. "I am small," he replied.

Before that there was an enquiry about whether, if they answered a call of nature, it would be transmitted. It would be, as Susannah's upright technique, with shorts on, caused hilarity among the boys who could not believe what they had witnessed. "Have you never seen a woman urinate," asked Susannah indignantly. "Not standing on a log out at sea," replied John. After five hours, Bridget and Helen indicated they were coming off the log. Helen realised there was no way she could stay out as long as the others if they were planning to be out there for at least a day. Bridget mentioned to Helen that they had no need to stay on the log because they were not in any danger of being voted off the next evening, so it was only the boys who needed to be there. "The reason those four are staying up there is because they know they're the next off,' is how Jonny remembers it. He told the others. Bridget then repeated the remark to Mark as she sat down for her steak. This caused fury among those left on the log, in particular Bridget's former tribe mates. They could not believe she could be so brazen. They launched into a diatribe against her, while an interested Alastair drank in every word. Bridget claims she did not mean the boys were the only ones who needed immunity, and John, Jonny and Susannah forgave her as soon as they came off the log after seeing how trivial a comment it was. But at the time they were incandescent with anger. As Susannah points, out she was in little danger of being voted off but she still tried her best to stay on the log as long as possible.

"When Helen and Bridget went, I said, 'What is this? Is it survival of the weakest?' It was ridiculous that all the strongest people should be voted off. This idea that she and Helen were invincible was stupid. We all started talking about how no one who had the stamina to stay on the log should go straight away. We weren't very nice about Bridget, which was to give Alastair some ammunition. Bridget wound the boys up more than she wound me up. I also think I'm more tolerant than they are. They spark off each other as well, just for laughs. I joined in because I was so angry. Of course, it gave Alastair ammunition, which he used later, to little effect, though."

Alastair was disadvantaged in some ways when Helen and Bridget left. He was now up against three South Island members, all supporting each other while no one was there to offer him encouragement. The other three members of his tribe had managed six and a half hours between them. The whole strategy for South Island from that moment on was to stop Alastair winning. "We knew we'd be there for ages because we knew Alastair wasn't going to jump in early on," remembers John. "I knew we were going to vote for Alastair but I didn't think they would vote for me. In my modesty, I thought they would vote for Jonny. It's a bit of a compliment that they wanted me off first. I knew Alastair was so full of shit. He wanted to stay there as long as he could. Towards the end, we wore him down psychologically. He knew he couldn't last as long as Jonny because Jonny actually enjoyed standing on the log. He was saying things like, 'I think I could get to 30 hours easily.' I said to him, 'You don't have to psych me out. I'm in an alliance with you.' He was talking about how fresh he felt."

The bitterness over Bridget's comment lasted for some time. "Imagine if those two won it. It'd be a travesty," was just a sample comment. It was generally accepted that Bridget and Helen were the weakest and that they were the least deserving. Alastair stood up for Helen as a "lovely girl" but accepted that she had done little while on the island. The idea of some sort of deal was starting to germinate. They all agreed it would be unfair if someone who had stood out on the log for longer than the others would then be voted off only a few hours later. As darkness descended the conversation continued in this vein. Finally, they were distracted. Susannah asked Jonny what his girlfriend would be doing while he was away. "Decorating," he answered. "If she's got the time between all that shagging around," added John. Susannah had already gone well past the record for a woman in such a challenge, a meagre six hours, held by Eve in Series 1.

As midnight approached, John and Jonny started to indulge their liking for music trivia, knowing well that Alastair had no interest in it whatsoever. They hoped that he would get bored and jump off, though John recognises that was unlikely, given the Scot's determination and fierce competitive instinct.

Drowning out the sound of passing aeroplanes, Series Editor Ed Forsdick reads the riot act to Tayfun after his smuggling antics at Bocas airport on day one.

Unused to handling large swords, Tayfun unsheathes the machete before proving that a Cambridge degree is not what it used to be.

A crestfallen Susannah tries to explain her mistake on the assault course to Sarah.

The photographer manages to capture the only time that South Island got their canoe to go in a straight line. Seconds later it hit a mud bank.

John makes an early, bold bid for ITV's new talent show, Give 'Em Enough Rope, *in which members of the public wittingly make complete fools of themselves on camera.*

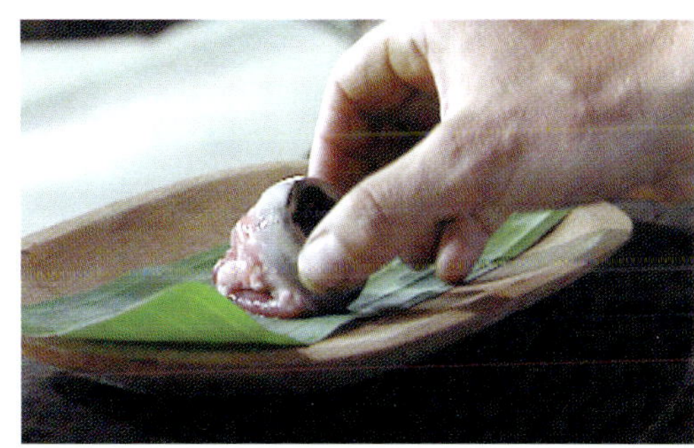

"It's the size of a baby's head." Fresh fish eyeball is the delicacy of the day.

John savours the full flavour of the sea as the eyeball explodes at the back of his throat.

Alastair's table manners leave a lot to be desired as he tackles the dreaded eyeball.

Drew Agger

Dave Porter

Meeta Bose

Tayfun Kadioglu

Helen Carney

Alastair Brogan

Jonny Gibb

Susannah Moffat

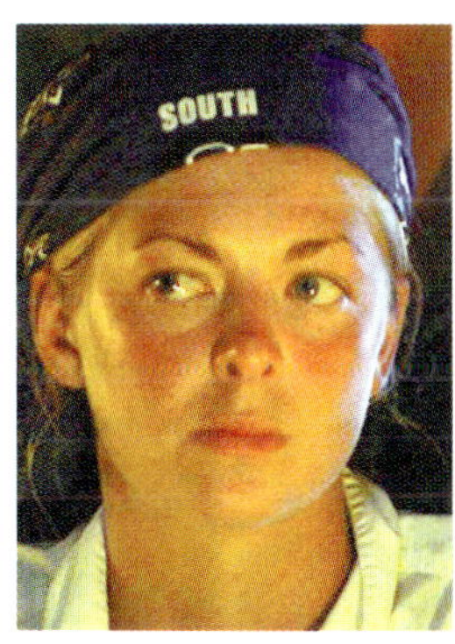

John Dalzell

Sarah McCombie

Lee Capon

Bridget Griffiths

*"Oh sh*t!" Dave falls off the log after just half an hour, despite fancying his chances of winning the challenge because "I always stand up in the pub, like."*

Dr Graham Johnson helps patch up Bridget's wounds after the Assault Course challenge.

"But I never got a chance to ask him who scored the goals." Mark Nicholas consoles an emotional Dave after he was unable to look his son Robert in the eye during the Family Values challenge.

"Where was the Mung Bean Salad, Barnaby?" Susannah thanks her husband for the care package after winning a phone call home in the Fallen Comrades challenge.

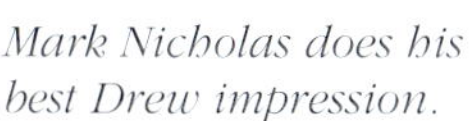

Mark Nicholas does his best Drew impression.

The last two standing, Jonny and Susannah, discuss tactics, the contents of their speeches and, more importantly, their outfits for the final show.

A fully ablaze Tribal Council, as designed by Iain Andrews and his art department, awaits the two finalists.

"Lads and lasses of the jury." Dave takes the stand to grill the two finalists, watched intently by his five fellow angry men and women.

They believed he was trying to dislodge them by constantly rocking the log whenever one of them bent down to take their weight off their feet, or pick up a water bottle. His feet were so big, claims John, that he could shake the log simply by transferring his weight. John twice helped his rivals – first Jonny, then Alastair – from toppling into the sea by steadying them with his hands. A "No Touching" rule does exist for the log stand, but because it was created to deter contestants from pushing others in, after consideration Ed Forsdick decided to let it go.

Through the night the challenge continued. People started to hallucinate. Susannah thought she saw a scuba diver in the water. Then she saw a man with a cloak standing on the log. Everyone was on their guard against the momentary lapse in concentration that would cause them to lose balance and fall in. To keep exhaustion at bay they carried on talking; Susannah revealed that she left her wedding to the music from *Star Wars*; Alastair revealed that he bought his suits from Marks and Spencer; Jonny spoke of his desire to beat Andy's record; John tried to remember the words to the theme tune of *Top Cat*. All of a sudden the rain came pouring down, just to set the seal on an uncomfortable night. Susannah spoke of jumping in but was urged by Jonny to stay to watch the sun rise at least. People started to edge away from Alastair when he revealed that he had killed his sister's goldfish when he poured perfume into its bowl. He also revealed a few facts about his real job and status – and the fact that he lives in a 300-year old castle. This was information he had still not revealed in full to his own tribe.

From then on, in the wee small hours of the morning, it was the desire to see the dawn that kept everyone going. All through the night they expressed the conviction that it was wrong for any of them to be voted off. At around 6am, cracks of light starting appearing in the night sky and slowly dawn broke, a wondrous sight for very tired Survivors. John and Alastair's feet started showing signs of swelling badly, though Jonny's were coping fine. Shortly after 7.51am Susannah decided she had had enough and it was time for breakfast. She gingerly climbed in to the water so as not to disturb the log. Hers had been an astonishing achievement of more than 17 hours, of which she is rightly very proud. Amazingly, she claims she could have gone on longer.

"I managed 17 hours and I felt I wanted to give my support to the boys and I also wanted to stand there as long as I could, for my own personal esteem. The longer I lasted, the better chance we had of breaking Alastair. He was wobbling the log constantly, trying to get us off. He was talking all the time but the boys were trying to psych him out with their media pop quiz, which was also doing my head in. It was a test of endurance just listening to them. One thing that was good was how they kept me going and how they supported me. At 3am Jonny said to me, 'You can't go in now. You've at least got to last until sunrise.' I wish I had been standing on the other side to see how well they were doing. I didn't know how much bravado there was. My feet were fine and I could have stayed on for longer but I reasoned that the longer I stayed on, the longer Alastair would. No way would he go before a woman. No way at all. By staying on, I thought I was upping the ante and the longer he would stay."

Back on the log, the politics started. The three agreed that none of them should be voted off. Alastair suggested, or so John and Jonny claim, that they should vote for Helen while his tribe should vote for Susannah. There was no way John or Jonny were going to have that after the effort she had just put in and they told Alastair that, so he suggested Bridget. Slowly but surely, a deal was brokered.

"After 21 hours, Alastair started talking about what a shame it was that we would have to go head-to-head at the Tribal Council," recalls John. "I can't remember who suggested that there was another way – that we just vote for other people and convince them to vote for the weakest and not the strongest. It just seemed unfair that we would have stood there so long and that we would be voted off that night. He agreed and said he would put it to them. We were angry with Bridget, and it seemed so futile afterwards, but at the time we were furious, that she was belittling our achievement. Susannah didn't think she had to be there but she still stayed on as long as she could. Nothing was really mentioned then, though and I became resigned to the fact I would not win it but I wanted to make sure Jonny won it because if Alastair did then I would be voted off. Alastair was very sneaky. He would rock the log. His feet were so big and he would twitch them and rock the log whenever Jonny bent down to take the weight of his feet. I told him to stop doing it at the end. He was trying all the psychological warfare stuff. He would say things like, 'I've got a second wind, I think I might just win this.' After about 21 hours he agreed he could not beat Jonny. He was really untrustworthy. Despite that, he made a deal. I said I wanted to do 24 hours, just to beat Andy's record. We knew Jonny could go on and on because his feet were fine whereas Al's and mine were really swollen. We kept telling Alastair how bad his feet were and we managed to talk him into a worse state than he really was. When it got near the end Jonny got really nervous and started shaking. I think Alastair hoped he would fall in and I would then give up."

Alastair claims that he did not suggest Helen's name to John and Jonny, but they are adamant that he did. Jonny says, "We were surprised that he mentioned Helen because he seemed to get on so well with her, but he was prepared to sell her down the river. Her name came up after Susannah went. Alastair was still talking crap about what he did for a living – he said he'd only been at the job for six months and he only got it because an older guy wasn't up to the job any more. He was talking pish, even after 21 hours on a log. I think he accepted I was going to win but he still hoped I would fall in because I had the odd wobble. But I said to Alastair, 'The only time I will come off this log is when I collapse and not beforehand.' He said to me afterwards that that comment had completely out-psyched him. But I meant it, totally."

Alastair accepts that he had no chance of beating Jonny given the latter's determination. But knowing that he had assured his safety was enough. He could return to his tribe and try to sell the deal to them, knowing he had some useful information about their view of Bridget that he might employ at a later stage. "Hopefully my tribe wasn't pissed off that I was speaking on their behalf. I didn't want to. I threw in a comment to them and they dwelled on it. They were pissed off with Bridget. Five hours in, Bridget and Helen jumped off and they were being interviewed by Mark and what was overheard was that Bridget said, 'I don't have to stand on the log because I'm not the one who needs immunity. I'm safe and they're the ones who need to be careful,' that is, John and myself. My God, did she get abuse from Susannah, John and Jonny. They hounded her and gave her so much stick. I just threw in the comment, 'Well, guys, we're all voting for John and you're all voting for me, we can change this if you want.' Later on, John or Jonny made the comment that it was ridiculous that John and I would be voted for after spending so much time on the log. I agreed and it was a case of 'how about you voting for someone else, the weakest person, and we'll do the same and we'll allow them to go head to head rather than John and me'. I said it was up to them, in the hope that one of them might even vote for Bridget, which was a bit naïve, though they were very pissed off with her. They said 'Fine' and John asked if I could convince my tribe and I said, 'They're free-thinking people but I will put it to them.'

"I said I would put it to Drew, Helen and Dave and see what they would say. Yes, I was saving my skin, no question about it. They wanted two others to go head-to-head and the way I thought about it was that they didn't have anything to gain from that because at the end of the day all we were doing was saving ourselves and putting somebody else up for it. I thought we could get rid of Bridget, maybe on the second vote they might switch to Bridget and trust us as a tribe. That would have been a better solution. I did not know who they were going to vote for, though I had an inkling that it wasn't going to be Dave."

At 2.38pm, John and Alastair decided to jump in and swam to the shore. After a quick chat with Mark they turned and summoned Jonny, who dived into the water, a gleeful smile on his face. He was delighted. Since day one he had set his heart on winning this challenge and he had done so in the most dramatic and remarkable way. It had been a true display of character, mental strength and determination. For such a tough competitor as Alastair to back down as he did shows how vehement Jonny's will to win was. He could quite easily have gone on longer; indeed, he says he fully expected to. He would not have flinched from going through another night, unless exhaustion set in, which he felt was unlikely. As an undercover police officer, he is used to working long shifts, even days on end when there has been a big drug bust under way. He was a worthy breaker of Andy's record, which had not just been broken once, but shattered three times. All three could be proud of their contribution and the humorous, often hilarious, way they had coped with the most trying circumstances.

There was little time for them to savour their achievement because Tribal Council was only a few hours away and tactics had been reversed. Once back on their island any notion of getting any rest was disregarded in favour of trying to sell their deal to their tribe mates. Hoping to arrive back to a volley of roses and a heroes' welcome, they were disappointed to find no one there; they were all out fishing, even Helen had been persuaded to go by Susannah, who had grabbed only a few hours sleep after her efforts on the log. Helen's indolence did her few favours. When the fishing party returned, the former tribes gathered for huddled discussions.

Alastair told his tribe what the score was. "After 24 hours on the log, what we've decided to do is this: they're not going to vote me off; they're not going to vote for me, full stop. They are going to vote for somebody who they feel – and they are not even telling me who this is – is weakest. You can do completely as you please, but I am not going to vote for John any more. I'm going to vote for somebody I want off and it's going to be Bridget." Alastair, of course, was being disingenuous. He went on to tell his tribe he had no idea who they would select to vote off. He knew they were going to vote for Helen, even if he did not put her name forward. To say to them, 'You can do as you please,' may have been correct but the fact was they would be hurting themselves to do so. He had presented them with a fait accompli. If they still decided to vote off John then the most he would garner was three votes, while Helen would receive four votes if the former members of South Island stuck together. They would then be at a disadvantage and be picked off. There was also very little time for anyone to devise a counter-plan, there being only an hour or so before they set sail for Tribal Council. Alastair's excellent salesmanship had won the day – just.

Dave was unhappy with how Alastair had decided to change their game plan without consulting them. He suspected that Alastair had formed an alliance with the two Johns. He felt if John and Jonny wanted Bridget off as much as Alastair claimed they did, then why did they not just vote her off themselves? But John and Jonny did not want to be part of the weaker tribe. In spite of his reservations, Dave had to go along with Alastair's plan. Drew was not 100 per cent convinced, but claims there was little she could do. "I was surprised when we found out that Al had changed the whole game, if you like," she says. "We did not expect the game to change because it had been so predetermined. It was big news and a bit of a shock but I totally understood where he was coming from straight away. What they had done on the log was amazing. And there was the whole thing with Bridget, which I didn't hear, but the gist of it was that she felt she didn't have to stay on the log because she was perceived as a weaker person who didn't have to work so hard anyway. Al was positive that he wasn't going to vote for John and because Al wasn't going to vote for John and we knew it was going to be a 4-4 draw then we'd be kicking ourselves in the head if we decided still to vote for John."

Surprisingly, given that she was the one who suffered, Helen was sanguine about the whole deal and does not blame Alastair for hastening her demise to save his own skin. "We were all gobsmacked but we did not have to accept it. Before those lads came off, we had all discussed it back at the camp and decided it was not appropriate to vote them off, especially after all the effort they had put in, and that includes Susannah. That only left Bridget from South Island. If we were to have still voted for

John then we would have lost because Al said he wouldn't vote for him so we would have lost 4-3. I did not know they were going to vote for me. They said they wanted to vote for the weakest person, which they perceived to be me. Physically, I was probably the weakest, though I thought they might go for Drew. We were shocked that Alastair changed the game because before then we had decided everything as a group. But there was little we could do because it was Tribal Council in half an hour."

Amongst the former South Islanders, Susannah was in swift agreement with the proposed deal. "According to John and Jonny, Alastair selected Helen from his tribe, which was ironic because they were very close. That really surprised all of us. Apparently, his first suggestion was that I go up against Helen, which in hindsight would have not have been too bad because I would have a got a few of the survival questions right. But they persuaded Al to vote for Bridget. Ultimately, everyone took a step back from the game and left it up to fate. Whoever won, their tribe would have an upper hand." Bridget felt the same and had become fatalistic. It seems standing on a log for a day is a sure-fire scheme to get your own way. "I wasn't bothered," she says now, "because there was little I could do. Had we voted for Alastair, then with me up against Alastair, I would have lost. Especially with it being a quiz. I approached that Tribal Council, thinking 'If this is it, then this is it.' I would have got to merger, got on the jury and reached as far as I hoped. I accepted that and prepared for it."

Tribal Council was extremely tense because everyone knew that, if tribal loyalties remained strong and established alliances held firm, then the outcome of the whole contest hinged on what would happen that night at the Tribal Council. It was also a novelty for *Survivor,* where usually the strongest go first, rather than the weakest. Predictably, the first vote was four for Bridget, four for Helen. Mark then asked Bridget and Helen each to make a short speech in their own favour, explaining why they should not be voted off. Their words made no difference: the pair, not being allowed to vote, each had three votes against them on the second ballot. Therefore, Mark announced, a survival quiz would be held to decide who stayed and who went. Neither Bridget or Helen had done any rigorous survival study or training and were consequently at sea with all of the questions. Susannah would probably have been best, followed by Alastair, who claims he would definitely have got two right, which would have beaten Bridget, and John and Jonny.

Everyone looked on agog as Mark read the five vital questions.

1. **Q:** Lumberman's, Star and Teepee are all types
of what?

    A: Fires

    (Helen: Shelter. Bridget: Tent)

2. **Q:** How might the bark from the Quinine tree
help you in Panama?

    A: As a malarial preventative

    (Helen: Itching, Bridget: Malaria – correct)

3. **Q:** What point on a compass lies between North
East and East?

    A: East North East

    (Helen: NNE, Bridget: NNE)

4. **Q:** A blast and a squirrel-tail are all types of what?

    A: Shelters

    (Helen: Tree, Bridget: Bird)

5. **Q:** A heliograph uses which natural source to
send a rescue signal?
A: The sun
(Helen: Heat, Bridget: Heat)

Bridget had one correct answer; Helen none. She collected her rucksack and left, and with her the likely chances of Drew, Alastair and Dave. South Island, and Bridget in particular, were delighted. For them, the reality was that the winner would come from their number. Jonny was aware of the significance immediately. "It was brilliant when Bridget won because now I knew there was a very good chance we would make the final three because we were so tight," he says. For a different reason, John was also delighted. "We were quite glad to see Helen go because her swearing got quite gratuitous and you don't want to hear someone walking around shouting, 'I've just had a right good shit.' "

There were some reservations among former North Island members about how the tribal council had been decided, mainly Helen herself, The questions were bona-fide survival questions, dredged from books and the internet and checked and checked again. But the simple fact is, as Alastair accepts, there was no other way. It is all right to criticise the quiz as unfair or an unsuitable way to decide something so important, but not unless you have a better answer. Helen's only complaint was that it was not about what they had learned on the island. "The quiz was weird. We had no idea how they would decide between us. There wasn't much more they could do, other than a quiz. I thought the questions would be based roughly on the people, the area and names of the islands, instead of things that were completely unrelated to *Survivor*. They were like SAS-style questions. I thought it might be about what we have picked up on the island. I wasn't pissed off; it was more like 'Game Over.' I was surprised because am I quite competitive. I loved being on the jury – though I missed being on the island and taking part in the challenges.

"I did feel guilty for quite a few days afterwards. I felt responsible for my tribe then being picked off because I didn't know the answer to the questions. But I felt better when the others came off and Drew and Dave said they wouldn't have got any right. It was difficult to bear." It's not as if Helen has never undergone survival training; before embarking on a youth development programme for Operation Raleigh in Belize aged 18, she was trained in "jungle awareness" for a week. But it did not help her. She has a sense of grievance about the questions, complaining they weren't relevant and the survival books she read did not answer them. Had the questions been too easy, there would have been equal criticism and there had already been a challenge, the Ambassador's Visit, that dealt with questions about the tribe members. All the other contestants agreed this was a fair way of deciding who should be ejected. Better then flipping a coin, anyway.

As for Alastair, did he wish that he had not made the deal and gone head-to-head with John? "There was an element of thinking, 'If I had gone head-to-head with John, who would have won? I could have won.' I asked John the question about how many he would have got right and he said, 'One'. I would have got two out of five, I'm certain. I would have got the heliograph and the northeast and I may have got the one about the fire, perhaps. But who knows what might have happened. I think it wouldn't have changed the game for me because my lot would've voted me off. They told me when they got on the jury that they would have got rid of me sooner than later. If Helen had won then she, Dave and Drew would have voted me off first. I asked Dave what he would have if I had gone to him and said, 'Let's vote Helen off.' He said he would have voted me off, so I sit with a great deal of comfort that I would have not got much further. But there is an element of guilt over what happened to Helen."

When they got back to their beach, the mood was reticent. South did not feel like gloating over what had happened – no mention was made of the numerical advantage they had over North, not yet – especially Bridget. She felt uneasy, in the same way that all people do when they have endured a near miss, as if it could and should have been them. People consoled themselves with the thought that Helen would enjoy being on the jury: they were right. She was taken to the Buccaneer where she was fed and watered and from then on had the chance to sit in the sun drinking beer for the next two weeks. She ate and drank so much that she ended up putting back on all the weight she had lost in her time on the islands, if not more.

The next morning, day twenty-one, and the remaining former members of North Island were understandably demoralised. Drew described the events of the night before as "pretty rubbish"; Dave, sentimental as any Geordie, bemoaned the loss of his "little diamond", while Alastair, his feelings tinged with guilt, said he was "shattered". He consoled himself and his cohorts by explaining to them that he believed the deal on the log extended beyond the previous evening. According to him, Jonny and John wanted to see how the game would pan out at 4-4, and leave it to the rules. Now that Helen had gone he thought they would, because of all the things they said about her on the log, vote off Bridget. They had not voted her off the night before, he told the camera, because they were concerned North would not be true to their word and not vote them off one by one. Now they had the advantage, he felt the deal was to get rid of Bridget, regain parity at 3-3 and then the game would begin again on a level playing field. Dave understandably had his doubts about whether South would honour their word, if indeed that was their word. John says no such deal was ever made. According to him, Alastair approached him that morning.

"Can I have word with you?" he said.

"Yes," John replied.

"As a mark of respect for our agreement out on the log, you should now vote off Bridget and bring us back to parity at 3-3."

"I don't remember that being part of the bargain. No."

"It was a gentleman's agreement that we wouldn't vote for each other."

"But that applied to last night only. It didn't apply thereafter."

That was not going to be the end of it, however. Alastair resolved there and then to do all he could to stay in the game. "Where there's breath, there's life" became his motto. But first there was a Reward Challenge. They were taken to the Spider Cave on the main island, a dank grotto filled with bats and a variety of spiders. This was not a game to suit the arachnophobes among the contestants – Jonny, Susannah and Drew. Had it been an Immunity Challenge then they might have attempted to conquer their fear. As it was, none of them collected a single spider. One person who believed this was her chance of winning a challenge was Bridget. She was far out in front and going well when she fell coming out of the cave and split her knee open. As the medic stitched her, writhing in agony on the floor, John went on to win. Worse to bear than the pain for Bridget was the knowledge that her fall had cost her a precious victory and the consequences of the injury meant it was unlikely she could compete in the other challenges. Her dream of just one victory, "to make my father proud", had deserted her. She was inconsolable.

"I was doing brilliantly. I had five or six spiders and I was running back into the cave, in front, but I was getting tired. I went flat on my face. The rocks under the water were loose. I put my foot on one. My lamp went out and I was trying to catch spiders without my lamp. Susannah said 'have my lamp'. I was told to go out and get my lamp lit and as I walked outside I saw a stream of blood going down my leg. I thought, 'They won't let me go back in there.' I started crying. God, it hurt."

She was given a salve when John, recognising that Bridget would have won, decided to share his reward, a night of luxury, with her. In an ideal world he would have taken his mate Jonny, but he knew Bridget deserved it. The prize was wonderful, and fulfilled Bridget's long-held need to feel clean. Not someone to be precious about being dirty, she was surprised how obsessive she got about being clean while on the island. Even after leaving the island and joining the jury, she was still washing her hands constantly. She is full of praise and thanks to John for his generosity.

"That evening was one of the highlights of *Survivor* for me because I felt honoured that John chose me. He and Jonny agreed while I was being patched up to give me the reward because they knew I would have won it. I was in floods of tears. Even Ed had tears in his eyes. It was a lovely reward: lobster, wine, fruit, meat and cheese. We couldn't eat it all, though we gave it a good shot. We had all the soap, shampoo, conditioners as well. I had forgotten what it was like to smell nice. Every now and then one of the girls would walk past from the crew and you could smell deodorant or face cream and I would follow the smell around. It was so lovely. It was the first time I've ever slept in a hammock. I slept well; John didn't. He moaned all the time. He didn't like the hammock, he was bitten and he didn't like all the noises around. The security guard sleeping nearby bothered him as well. Occasionally the guard would flash his torch and wake John up. John's not a wuss – he's a fuss. He's a hard man to please. The next morning I washed my clothes in the water with my shampoo. Then we had breakfast: Danish cinnamon pastries, coffee – I loved it. I went back to the island beaming, though I trod carefully so that no one thought I was gloating."

Walking Wounded

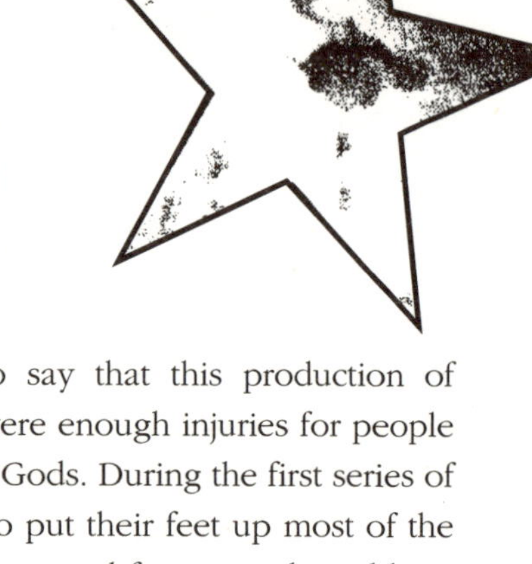

It would be going a bit far to say that this production of *Survivor* was cursed, but there were enough injuries for people to cast a suspicious glance at the Gods. During the first series of *Survivor*, the medics were able to put their feet up most of the time. The most serious injuries stemmed from people stubbing their feet, and that was remedied by the slaughter of a goat by a Bornean witchdoctor seeking to appease the island spirits. On Bocas, however, the injuries came thick and fast and few of the contestants escaped a wound of some sort. At times it was like a scene from *M.A.S.H.*

Bridget suffered the most serious injury – except for Dave's "funny turn" during Hands-up – when she slashed open her knee during the Spider Cave Reward Challenge. She then burst open the stitches during the ill-fated Hands-up Reward and required more stitches. Her knee had already begun to heal when she re-opened the wound so Mark Dawes, one of the three medics on stand-by, had to insert a gloved finger into the wound to start the bleeding afresh and restart the healing process from scratch. At one stage it was thought that she would have to be withdrawn from the game for fear of infection, but a mixture of luck and cussed bravery on her part meant that she carried on.

Dave, again, was in the wars when he cut his foot before the swimming relay. A nasty gash was made worse when the sand got in the wound and gouged away flesh, creating a small hole the size of a pea through to the bone. Once again, there was concern that he would need to be flown off the island and out of the game for treatment, but daily dressing by the medics ensured that the risk of infection was contained, though the existence of injuries like the one affecting Dave meant that, when merger was reached, a tarpaulin was awarded to the contestants to prevent infection setting in. The medics are full of praise for the way Dave uncomplainingly dealt with his injury, despite the great pain and discomfort it caused him.

Little John's foot was another casualty. At some stage shortly after merger a thorn or some similar object cut his foot and because of the conditions it instantly went black and looked nasty. Thankfully, the wound did not need to be scoured and a course of antibiotics prevented any serious infection. He also cut his leg badly rampaging through the jungle on the "Orientation Island" challenge. Just as John recovered from that, however, he was laid low by tonsillitis, picked up from Susannah, and this was still affecting him after he returned to Winchester and required a hospital visit.

Among the other injuries were Drew's black eye when Jonny guided her into a wooden beam during the "Balancing Beams" challenge; Susannah cut her leg when climbing into the boat; everyone else was bitten by sand flies and mosquitoes, scarring their limbs, and contracted blisters and other sores.

Injuries weren't confined to the contestants: Technical Director Peter Johnston broke his nose after falling on a boat turned vertical by high seas; underwater cameraman Jason Isley fell playing football and bit through his lower lip when his face hit an opponent's knee, requiring several stitches; another cameraman, Richard Farrish, dislocated his shoulder playing pool and had to be flown home. Alongside these more serious injuries, there were all the various stomach complaints and maladies that are part of such a large production.

So, on behalf of all the contestants and crew, thanks must go to medics Dr Graham Johnson, Mark Dawes and Andy Thurgood, all of whom certainly earned their keep.

Week 4

Hit the North

The morning of day twenty-two, it was perfectly evident that Alastair had to win immunity if he was to remain on the island. He had hoped that the time he spent on the log with John and Jonny would give him an advantage with remaining members of South Island. He was wrong, however, as Jonny had made abundantly clear to camera the day before. While on the log, Alastair had not looked beyond securing his position on the island for the next three days. South Island members were worried that a swimming challenge would come along and that Alastair would win. Therefore they needed to get rid of him as soon as possible. As for making a deal with him, that was not going to happen either. "I don't trust him in the slightest," Jonny said. "I think that he will do whatever he possibly can to win the million pounds. I don't believe that he has come out for the experience. I think he's here solely to win the money." Not a criticism, just recognition that he was a formidable competitor and a danger to Jonny's chances of winning.

Understandably, given the importance of the next Immunity Challenge, Alastair was hardly exerting himself around the camp. It was noticed that he spent most of the time in the shelter gathering his strength. Again, this failed to endear him to South Island and hardened their view that he had to go. All four were as strong as ever, now that Bridget's comment had been forgotten and forgiven. What was important was that someone other than Alastair should win immunity. John returned from his night of luxury with Bridget feeling slightly excluded, paranoid even, surprised how just one night away had left him feeling out of the loop. He felt suitably invigorated for the challenge, though. Drew meanwhile wanted to go home, a state of mind that would have combustive results later in the day.

And for John it was an ideal challenge: an obstacle course on Lost Island, albeit one with a twist. Before tackling the course, the contestants were sat down and asked a series of questions. If they answered them correctly, they were able to hand 1kg bags of sand to the contestant they wished to handicap. There were five questions:

1. **Q:** Which Panamanian snake is not poisonous: bushmaster, fer-de-lance or vine snake?

    A: Vine Snake

    Drew, Alastair, Dave, John, Susannah, Bridget correct.

2. **Q:** Which metal is best for lighting fires: magnesium, sodium or aluminium?

    A: Magnesium

    Drew, Jonny, Alastair, Dave, John, Susannah correct.

3. *Q:* How many species of animal are unique to
Panama: 25, 125 or 325?

A: 125

Drew, Dave, Bridget correct.

4. *Q:* Which organ is the first to be hit by heat stroke:
liver, heart or brains?

A:. Liver

Nobody correct.

5. *Q:* What is a cat hole: latrine, shelter or snare?

A: Latrine

Nobody correct.

As expected, Alastair and John got the lion's share of the handicap; Alastair carrying 9kg of weight, John 7kg. North did not seem to have their strategy off pat. It was obvious that John was the big favourite, so it made sense to hamper him with all the bags and pray that Jonny was still not in the best fettle after his heroics on the log. Instead, they spread their bags too thinly. The obstacle course was not long but it was certainly challenging. However, even if every bag had been given to John, it is likely that he would still have won. He managed to get around the course in a staggering one minute and four seconds of sustained effort. Everyone gave it their all, including Dave who almost brained himself on the stand holding the immunity amulet as he collapsed over the line. Bridget, despite being offered the opportunity to sit this challenge out, was determined to give it a go for pride's sake and acquitted herself admirably. "I had to do it for two reasons: firstly for me, to prove I can do it. The second was my children; I wasn't going to let them down. I didn't want to be a martyr. I wasn't going to go all out and say, 'Sod my knee.' I wanted to take it slowly and I did do, but I wanted to finish it, even doing it with a stick. I still managed it less than three minutes." Her courage won her the respect even of Hash Shaalan, the contestants' security guard, soon to be seen in the forthcoming *Terminator 3* as Arnold Schwarzenegger's stuntman, who figured her time was good even for someone whose knee did not resemble a patchwork quilt.

No one gave it more than Alastair but he was played out, his strength gone. He went last and gave the course his absolute all. But being a big man was not ideal on such a course. "My feet had ballooned so much after the log challenge that I could barely fit them in my boots," he says. "I came third but John was unbelievably fast. Susannah, the bitch, gave me everything and I ended up with 9kg and I fell flat on my face three times because I knew I had to win. I don't think the handicap made that much difference. I don't think I could have beaten John, to be honest, even if I didn't have a pack on. I knew he was going to win. When I got up from going underneath one of the obstacles I put my leg down to pull myself up and it collapsed. It was the first time anything like that has ever happened in my life, even during all the time I played rugby. By the end the lactic acid had got into me so much that I had a feeling I had never had before. It was a combination of the stress, the nervousness, the need to win and not having proper food for 21 days. All that made such a massive difference to me. I was incredibly impressed with people like Drew and Dave and how they got round."

John, revelling in such an impressive victory, got carried away by his achievement. He had heard mention that the locals had beaten his time and he wanted to see if he could have another crack at it to beat their record. This struck the others, former North members in particular, as further evidence of his arrogance. They liked him and thought him funny but his

showing off on the bar on day six and on this occasion,
blackened his name for the time they joined the jury and would
have to vote for the person they believed to have the best
chance of winning. But John was relieved to have got
immunity for his tribe. "When we saw the assault course, I knew
I would win it. We walked the course and Alastair was asking
how much I weighed and the handicap I was carrying and he
was going, 'So pound for pound you are carrying much more
weight than I am,' referring to my body weight and it was all
that sort of psychological crap. I said, 'Yes, but for five years in
the Marines I used to do 30 mile runs with 30lb on my back. I
knew I would win because it came to speed and how nimble
you could be. We had to get rid of him."

On the way back to Isla Popa on the boat Drew dropped
her bombshell. Realising she was a sitting duck and that her
destiny was in other people's hands, she had got fed up and
wanted off the island. She approached John, seeing him as the
leader of the former South Island faction, and asked if he would
vote her off instead of Alastair. If they did not, she warned, then
she would not vote for John, should he reach the last two and
she would also do her best to be destructive and unhelpful
around the camp and, more pointedly, would destroy food.
John was shocked. "I felt like Elliot Ness with Al Capone. I
received more threats in ten minutes than I'd had in the rest of
my life," he joked. John told her that he would not personally
change his vote and that he would not bow to threats. When
John told this to the others, including Dave, they could not
believe she would be so vindictive. The feeling was that Drew
had gone too far. Had she asked reasonably to be voted off
next, then her request would have been considered. As it was,
it was dismissed out of hand. She regrets what she said and how
she handled it.

"We knew we were going to be picked off one by one and

Alastair knew he was next," she maintains. "I knew he didn't want to go and I knew that the next person to go after Ali would be me. This was all predetermined; everyone knew it. I felt that if I could persuade South Island – bearing in mind that I knew I was going and could do little about it, there was no way of getting in with South Island or winning every immunity – rather than me having to hang around here for another three days with no food, getting weaker, would it be OK if I went before him? They were adamant that they wanted Ali to go because they were worried that a swimming challenge might be coming up and he's an exceptional swimmer.

"I know it sounds really bad, threatening to destroy the food, but it was not something I intended to do. It was just a last desperate attempt to get them to vote me off. I wouldn't say I had lost my will to fight; I was merely facing up to reality. I really just wanted to go. John was shocked and told the others and they were absolutely horrified that I could suggest it. Looking back, I'd be just as horrified. Even Dave was upset, which is saying something. Even in spite of all of that, they still wanted Ali off first, so the whole thing completely blew up in my face. I upset everybody and it caused me a bit of a hoo-ha for a bit. Everyone was pissed off with me and I can totally understand that. Then eventually we all talked about it. Funnily enough, that served to clear the air and after that the tribe worked a lot better together."

Susannah, John and Jonny all sensed that Alastair might be behind this somehow. During the boat ride back from the challenge he had been seen whispering conspiratorially with Drew, shortly before she addressed John. Then, when Drew's threats were commonly known and the whole tribe confronted her, Alastair spoke in her defence. Susannah feels he was the mastermind. "Alastair spoke for Drew. He explained how she felt and why she had said it. She did not say a word the whole time he was explaining. It seemed to us that, even if he hadn't been the brains behind the plan and it was initiated by her, he did not mind her saying what she did. I don't think Drew had thought through what she had said. So Alastair stepped in. He was one for taking control and overpowering the conversation. He tried to persuade us it would be a kind thing to do for Drew. Even if it was not his idea, then he was not averse to trying to use what she said to his advantage, to buy himself more time." As a result of the opprobrium heaped upon her for her comments, particularly from Dave, Drew burst into tears when she realised it had all been a complete waste of time and only served to alienate her from the others.

Alastair categorically and emphatically denies playing any part in Drew's outburst. Indeed, he claims he was upset because in the resulting brouhaha, she let slip that Alastair and the others were considering confronting Bridget and telling her the comments made about her on the log and so gave away his last-ditch plan to stay on the island.

"On the way back, the shit hit the fan. Drew sat with me on the boat and knew I was going. I said to her that I was going to speak with John, who's got a lot of integrity. Jonny not so much, he looks away, never meets your eye, plays things down a bit. I said that if I were to ask John tomorrow, then he would tell me whether I am going to be voted off. Drew said she wanted to go first, that she didn't want to be there any more. I told her to leave it until I had spoken to John. As she was getting off the boat she said she was going to tell John then. I said that maybe it wasn't a good idea. But she went ahead and she brought up the slagging that Bridget got on the log. I could perhaps have convinced Bridget to swap sides if I'd told her what they had said. I made the decision not to do that because I thought Bridget would not believe me and that it wouldn't work. It would make me look desperate, a complete arse. I felt I had to back Drew and so in front of John and Jonny I said, 'John you did say a lot of things' and I said my piece because I didn't want to get embroiled and I didn't want to go down that road."

The whole episode was like High Noon: the "Battle of Popa" as it will become known. Everyone had a go at Drew, while Alastair defended her honour stoutly. Alastair threatened to tell Bridget what they said about her on the log, verbatim, causing Jonny to shoot him a look of pure hatred. During all of this Bridget was blissfully ignorant, but hearing her name called she approached the group. "Have I upset Alastair in some way?" she asked Drew. Alastair stormed down to the creek.

Just to make sure that Alastair did not try to poison Bridget against the others and cut some deal with her, Susannah and Jonny called her behind the shelter so they could confess. They informed her of what they said on the log and that she should be wary of large Scotsmen bearing gifts and promises. Bridget maintained that she had said they were all fighting to stay on the island, not just the boys, and that she just felt it was the right time to get off the log because they had spent the whole day talking about how long they would last. As this conversation took place, Alastair came back and was told by Jonny that they were getting things out in the open. "No, no, no, let's just have our dinner and let's forget everything," he said, knowing the game was finally up and his plan of causing a schism in South Island was scuppered. "I want to be able to kiss and shake hands," he added.

"They were still talking about the whole thing when I got back," is the way Alastair remembers it. "John turned to me and said, 'Alastair, I think we should talk about what went on on the log, and get it out of the way.' I said no. I didn't want to talk about it; I said I wanted my last night in good humour and didn't want a bad atmosphere. They were going to put their side of the story to Bridget but I fluffed it over and they tried to bring it back up again a couple of times and I refused to talk about it. Eventually, John said 'fine' and we had a good night. I did think Bridget might have come to me and said, 'What was said?' But she's not like that and that was it and I was voted off. If I had done it, then it would have been the act of an incredibly desperate man but I weighed up the pros and cons and decided it wasn't me. That night off camera Drew burst into tears three or four times, realising how stupid she had been and what she had done. The next day when I was being voted off she cried again. I said 'goodbyes' in good faith. Jonny didn't look at me, John was OK, Susannah was false as ever. I find her very false. I have a feeling she doesn't mean a single thing she says."

Ironically, Alastair's view of Susannah was similar to the one that Jonny, John and Susannah held of him. John scoffs at Alastair's suggestion that he did not try any more skulduggery after the row over Drew's comments was sorted out. "He was still trying it on and scheming on the boat over to Tribal Council. I refused to accept he was actually going until I saw him put his torch out and walk down that path." Jonny had never trusted Alastair and was not going to alter his standpoint, especially after Drew's eruption after Tribal Council. "After the log challenge, John said he thought Alastair was all right. I said, 'No, I don't trust him one bit. He's a devious, lying bastard.' John was a bit taken aback. But when Alastair admitted on his last day what he did for a living and said how much he earned, I told John. He said, 'After that log challenge I thought Alastair was quite an affable guy and I was quite surprised how harsh you were. I thought you had got the wrong end of the stick. But it turns out you were right; he's a devious lying bastard.' He admitted he was a managing director on his last day and said he was one of three. He said he was on more than 100 grand a year," Jonny says, feeling his suspicion was justified.

Later that day Alastair, Dave and Drew, aware their time was drawing to a close, were debating the possible outcome. Both Dave and Alastair said they wanted to Jonny to win and that he would face John in the final two because he, the ex-Royal Marine, was capable of winning every immunity from there on in. Alastair then mentioned how much he was looking forward to seeing Helen and having a shave and a few beers. Contrary to what John thought, he was not speaking like a man with another plan in store. He sounded and looked like someone who had come to terms with the fact that he had lost and was going. This mood of defeatism definitely spread to Drew, who more people expected to be a fighter and go down kicking and screaming rather than whimpering and sulking.

That night, Alastair was allowed to hold court around the fire one more time, regaling everyone with his tales of sporting prowess. Drew had done her penance and was allowed to sort out the corn rations by Susannah, who – like the others –had previously had suspicions that Drew was cooking too much rice, because she was not concerned about rationing it once she thought she was going to be voted off. The conversation was easy and it appeared that the air had cleared. They even got on to discussing favourite films, reminding South Island members of their days of being the "Hampstead set". The only concern of the evening was when they thought that a snake had got in the tent, but it was a false alarm. John claimed he felt a pull at the tarpaulin, but it could well have been a fox that was sighted around the camp earlier, attracted by the chickens, which were one less in number after that night's meal. They all admitted that the day's events, when replayed on television might make them look like "arseholes", as Jonny put it, swearer-in-chief now that Helen had gone. "Even teachers can be pricks," admitted Susannah.

Susannah's view of Alastair was further discoloured when he returned from doing a piece to camera the next morning, day twenty-three. He had been asked about Jonny and Susannah's relationship and when he got back to camp, according to Susannah, he insinuated that the producers thought something was going on between them. On camera, when asked about their relationship, he said the bond was no stronger than his with Helen, or Dave's with Meeta. Returning to camp he then stirred things up by saying to Susannah that the producers were trying to make something of Jonny and Susannah's friendship. The pair maintain they were just good friends. Susannah was annoyed. In her interview on camera on day twenty-three she made a point of saying that Alastair was a troublemaker. There was little love lost between them. Both would be loath to accept it, but they are quite similar beneath the surface – tough, ambitious, confident and consequently seen by the others as manipulative and cunning. Perhaps that lay behind their indifference to each other. Susannah's problem was that, if she was to make the final two, then she would have to deal with the fact that Alastair would be on the jury with a number of his North Island cronies over whom his influence was extremely powerful. It is likely he would spend time singing the praises of John and Jonny while voicing his wariness of her. Prophetically, she told the camera on the day he left, "I do worry about him being on the jury and how manipulative he will be with others and whether he will try to sway people against certain people with whatever tiny jots of info he might have."

But at Tribal Council, Alastair had nothing up his sleeve and was voted off. Susannah was shocked by the three votes she received, making her realise how vulnerable she was. The million pounds was drawing ever closer and beginning to play on people's minds. Without Alastair there would be a release of tension, Dave and Drew being more passive and accepting than their leader had been. That said, everyone had respect for Alastair as a fierce and formidable competitor, which he had proved to be in the challenges, though disappointingly for him he had failed to win a single reward or an immunity. Rightly, he is flattered that he was voted off at that point. "I knew I would never win. I take it as a huge compliment. The bottom line was that I was voted off because I could win immunity. They didn't want to risk it. I can go with my head held high. My only guilt is what I did to Helen but she's told me not to worry about it. Only Dave was concerned about it."

In his post-Council interview with Mark Nicholas, Alastair spoke of his deep dislike of losing but how happy he was to be on the jury and still have some influence in who won. He tried to play the grey man but for someone of his charisma, energy, interpersonal skills and physique that was going to be virtually impossible. There are occasions when he might have engineered situations better for himself. Most obviously, he might have served himself better going head-to-head with a member of South Island, rather than Helen, but that is with the benefit of hindsight. Perhaps he should have not done a deal and instead gone all out to beat Jonny on the log. He figured he had another three or four hours in him, as did Jonny. It might well have gone into another night. But his main problem, in his opinion, came with losing the last two immunities before the merger and from then on he was always going to be a target. As he saw it, had they gone in at 5-3 he would have made the last four, then it would have been every man for himself. Asked how his epitaph would read, he said: "I would like to think that I played the game fair. I would like to think that the tribe members believed what I said and did was, A) honest and B) in their best interests. I haven't lost the million pounds; I just haven't won it."

Not so Dreary Drew

Day twenty-four came and people were beginning to feel the chronic lack of food. The rice was running low and had to be rationed accordingly. John spoke to the camera about how the lack of energy and the constant tension was making him emotional. "If someone made me sit down and watch *ET* or *The Champ*, I would just be drowning in my own tears." The low level of energy also lowered people's tolerance, he claimed. Interestingly, as someone who does not like being disliked, he found himself caring less about other people's opinions during the game. "I go out of my way to be liked by too many people and thereby lose a bit of my true personality. Since I have been out here I haven't cared too much about being liked. I have said one or two things to people … I don't care as much about being liked as playing the game fairly and straight so when you are hungry or tired it is difficult to care about who likes you and who doesn't."

Dave was also feeling lacklustre and was tired after any exertion of any sort. Living conditions were getting harder and harder and the energy to fish was lacking – as well as the skill. He expressed his frustration that the tribe was one in name only and that there were still two distinct groups. He had hoped that divisions might have broken down over time but he could see no way in which that could happen. Having made a tentative approach to John and Jonny, he realised there was no way he could join them. He was also already missing Alastair. "He was a smashing bloke," he said, as if he had died. "He was very fit, very strong. He had some stories to tell – you couldn't shut him up at times." His aim was to try to keep up Drew's morale and see if there was a way to join forces with Bridget and Susannah at the right time.

Susannah was suffering from stomach cramps due to hunger, the first time that had occurred. She was not aware of it then but she was also suffering the first symptoms of tonsillitis that would strike down her and then John. She echoed John's view about feeling emotional and vulnerable, particularly because of having votes stacking up against her. Unlike Dave, she was not missing Alastair. "He is an interesting guy with lots of stories to tell but he does tend to monopolise conversation. His stories go on for a long time and I am not saying that is a bad thing but you do notice the difference. There is a lot less military and armed forces talk around the place now, which I must say I am not missing an awful lot." Drew, she felt, was missing his influence, "because she doesn't know which way to go". She also talked about her choice of Shakespeare as her luxury item. "I realise that bringing that could possibly cause others to think I was arty-farty and precious." As a consequence, it had become very popular toilet paper, in an attempt to play down her literary pretensions.

While those three and Bridget sat around the camp, stomachs cramping and grumbling, Jonny and Drew were on a deep-sea fishing trip, the reward for winning that day's challenge, "Balancing Beams". Here the tribe was divided into random pairs, Jonny and Drew, Bridget and Dave and John and Susannah. Jonny and Drew were the best but whether that was a result of Drew's balance and agility or Jonny's navigational skills is a moot point. Whatever, it was only what Drew deserved after Jonny had guided her, blindfolded, into a beam, cutting her eye, another to add to the growing catalogue of injuries. While the crew got seasick, Jonny and Drew sat at the front of the boat necking beer and doing the odd spot of fishing for food later. They found they had a lot in common, Drew having been in the police force. She had enjoyed the job but needed a new challenge. Not being able to see herself doing the job for the next 10 years, she had decided to get out, realising she had to do it soon, rather than in a few years time when she was married and had kids. She met her boyfriend Robin and he told her what a great job the fire service is. The fact that Jonny's girlfriend, Ruth, was also a firefighter gave them something else in common. They had a fantastic time, as Drew remembers.

"I had never really got to know Jonny and we had a really good day, a really good laugh and talked about loads of things, 90 per cent of which was off-camera because the crew were feeling seasick. We talked about a lot of personal things. We were sitting at the front of the boat, and they were at the back and I would not have talked about half the stuff that we did had we been on camera. We talked about his girlfriend, my boyfriend, likes and dislikes – a whole load of stuff, helped by a load of beers. He said, 'Drew, I really feel as if I've got to know you. When I was in South Island I thought you were a miserable cow.' I said I was miserable and anxious and I know I can come across like that."

Jonny warmed so much to Drew that he began to doubt the plan to vote her off, ahead of Bridget, with whom he did not get on so well. "Drew said to me, 'I'd like to stay. But I just know there's no way I'm going to be able to win every immunity from now on in.' I said I would speak to John and see what he said and that I'd get back to her. John and I had both changed our minds about Drew and had begun to think there was a lot more to her than we thought originally, when she was just 'Dreary Drew' and we felt guilty about a lot of the things we said. I felt she deserved it because of her efforts in the challenge and personality-wise I had more in common with her than Bridget, or even Susannah."

When the pair arrived back at camp, the difference in Drew's demeanour was noticeable. Whereas before the trip she had been defeatist and passive, there was now a spring in her stride. John recognised what had happened immediately. "Drew got on really well with him and half fancied him, I think. When they went on that fishing trip, they had not really got on well before, but they came back best buddies. Jonny had worked his magic in 12 hours." Jonny approached him and put the theory forward that they should consider keeping Drew instead of Bridget because they liked her better. John, who could not stand Drew before the merger but had grown to like her, sympathised but would have nothing to do with it, as Jonny remembers. "He pointed out that Drew was fit, strong and she might win immunity and she might win the challenges. If she got in the final two, then she would win it because North would vote for her. If we voted Bridget off then there would be no way she would vote for us. I told Drew that we had agreed what we were going to do and we did not want to change that."

Drew took the news well, and claims there was nothing she could do to prolong her stay. She resolved just to enjoy what was left of her time on the island. "Jonny came back the following day and said that he had had a chat with John and John did not want to deviate from the original plan. I understood. It was what I was expecting to happen. I told him, 'You'll still get my vote at the end of the day.' It was a really nice thing that he had done that. It did occur to me, of course, to try to approach someone else to try and save myself. I wasn't going to approach Bridget because I knew I couldn't break her bond with the others. I didn't really like her and didn't want to pretend that I liked her. That would be false. Same thing with Susannah: I knew it wouldn't work."

Watching this going on with an interested eye was Susannah. Jonny also put the idea about keeping Drew to her but there was no way she was going to subscribe to it. She applauds Jonny's skill in being able to get on with everyone. While John and she were finding it difficult to be liked, to Jonny it came effortlessly. "Jonny is massively good at that," admits Susannah. "He's very, very sociable. I think it's part of his personality and part of his strategy for the game. He's gregarious and good at bringing people together. Drew asked Jonny if she could join our alliance and he said he would ask us. He spoke to us but we decided it was too late a stage in the game and it did not advantage us at all. Also, the day before or so she had gone funny, and we weren't sure that she could be entirely trusted."

Dave and Drew were finally made aware of Alastair's true story. Before leaving he had confessed to Jonny that he was Managing Director of a company and that if he cashed in his shares then he would be worth almost a million. Dave, as a result, felt a bit let down that Alastair had not been entirely truthful. "It just makes me wish that Drew and Helen had an independent voice and saw him for what he was," said Susannah, wistfully. "Alastair had a real hold on them and they did not seem to doubt him, whereas we never believed a word he said from the start. They thought he was looking out for them but really he was looking out for himself."

On day twenty-five, sick of having so little to eat and not being able to reach the coconuts, John broke the impasse by scaling one of the palms. Despite having lost so much weight and strength, he was still nimble enough to shimmy up the tree and grab three coconuts, resisting the opportunity to show off with a few chin-ups at the top – a sign for everyone that he was always going to be a formidable opponent in any challenge that involved physical fitness. Jonny told the camera that, if he, John and Susannah were to be the final three, he would take John through to the final two and not Susannah, whom he felt to be the more ambitious. He did not think John was there for the money, though he was, or at least he soon started to get interested in it as his chances of making the final three rose. He had earmarked the money for emigrating to Australia with his girlfriend and opening a physiotherapy clinic.

That morning with the Treemail there were sets of bows and arrows for them to practise with for that day's Immunity Challenge. The message with them read:

> *Practise away*
> *For your Challenge today*
> *Will be all about making your mark.*
> *Fail to take aim*
> *And the light from your flame*
> *Might tomorrow be plunged into dark.*

In practice no one was any good. Dave sensed, however, that here was a challenge that he could win. "I've never done it before in my life," he says. "Usually I didn't wear my glasses. They were my only pair so I kept them in the shelter. The bows were made from some tree on some island and some expert makes them, apparently, but it was like one of the bow and arrow sets you get from Woolworths. First try, it snapped in two. We got a few to practise with. I thought it'd be a farce. Eventually, I got it working. They got some kid – Mark said he was the King of Panama or something. This feller was shooting from the hip, like. We all missed in practice by miles. I think Ed was getting worried because the idea was that you hit one target and then aimed for another, smaller in size. But no one was hitting them. They brought the kid to show us. That worked and me and John got through. If this target gets any smaller, I thought, I'm going to have difficulty seeing it without me glasses. I could barely see the tree, never mind the target. I realised this was the best chance I had for an immunity so I didn't want to fluff it. I wanted to win one for my two lads. I was first and I had only had one chance – it went in. John missed. I was over the moon, dead chuffed."

The "kid" Dave spoke about was a cousin of the King of the Panamanian Indians, who constructed the bows out of the Pifar tree. Drew performed disappointingly in the challenge, to the point that Jonny thought she threw it on purpose because she was keen to go. "I didn't manage to hit it once. Jonny said to me, 'Did you try on that?' I can honestly say, hand on heart, that I did try and I didn't hit the thing once. I was useless. I got close but I lost. It was a very proud moment for Dave. I thought, 'Shit' but never mind. I had prepared myself for going and I knew if I had won it then I would have had to win the next one, and the one after that and after that. I knew, whatever happened, I would be the next picked off." Drew's disappointment meant joy for Dave, who finally had the challenge that would make his sons proud. He felt he was on a bit of a roll from that point on, an attitude that would have dramatic consequences on day twenty-seven.

The next morning Drew was up and packing her stuff at 9am. Obviously, she had no intention of making a last-minute attempt to try and stay. Given how badly her attempt to blackmail John went, it is hardly a surprise. Drew claims it is not in her nature to be snide or sneaky but one imagines that even if she tried she would not be very good at it. All she wanted to do was enjoy her last day by snorkelling and sunbathing. Dave was saddened by her imminent demise, knowing that he would be left to fly the North Island flag. He had not given up hope, though, and vowed to compete as hard as he could in every challenge. Both he, Drew and John noted how well Jonny was coping with the conditions compared to everyone else.

"I think Jonny is coping very well," John told the camera. "He is always happy, always got a sense of humour." He went on to say that, if no promises had been made, then he would have formed an alliance with Jonny, Dave and Drew in the final four. "Drew is funny, caring and generous and always has been. She's actually quite clever as well and that's something I never really gave her credit for before. I thought she was a wee bit slow on the uptake but she's not, by any stretch of the imagination. She's quite witty and funny and sharp and I've really warmed to her and Dave … I know I could strengthen my chances of winning the million pounds tenfold by voting Susannah off next rather than Drew but it's not something I am prepared to do. I don't want to seem like that and I don't want to play the game like that and it's just something I promised myself before I came out here: that I would play by a certain code and that's what I'm sticking by." When it was put to him that not taking the chance to vote off Susannah now would cost him down the line, even the chance of victory, he agreed. He did not know, but his chance of winning the million was drifting by and John, for all his sharp mind and incisive wit, was not clever enough to see it, or not machiavellian enough to act upon it. Jonny was willing to break their alliance to include Drew, but John wasn't.

On the way to the freshwater creek Dave took the opportunity to warn Jonny about Susannah. "I've got a funny feeling about her … I think that there is a sting in the tail there somewhere." Jonny took in what he was saying, or pretended to. Dave's theory seemed to be that because Susannah had been travelling she was not trustworthy and he did not believe she had given up her job to come here. "I reckon it's on hold," he added "She's not to be trusted." Whether Susannah had given up her job or not it appeared either was enough for her not to be trusted. The truth was that she had had to give up her job after her headmaster refused to give her six weeks off, for the understandable reason that it would disrupt the children's education. It was a wrench for her to leave the job, having just settled in and got to know the children. But there will be more teaching jobs in the future, or at least she hopes there will, whereas this would be her only chance to take part in *Survivor*. When she decided to leave, friends and colleagues were bewildered.

"I told them that I was leaving for personal reasons," she says. "One kid said, 'Miss, are you in trouble with the police?' Then word got around the school that perhaps I was pregnant. There were all these rumours. I said I would explain everything in due course. If anyone asked Barney where I was then I told him to say I had taken a school trip to Costa Rica. I was afraid that people would think I had left him and he was too embarrassed to admit it or that he had done me in and buried me under the patio." When the first show appeared on television, Mrs Moffat was spotted on TV and the official website was deluged with frantic e-mails from schoolchildren urging "Miss" on.

That night to no one's surprise Drew was voted off. The only eventful moment was an exchange between John and Mark Nicholas. "John,' asked Mark, "is there anything you WOULD do for more food?" After a ruminative pause, he answered, "Sexual favours." His interest pricked, Mark replied: "To whom?" Suppressing a grin, John shot back, "To you." Mark managed to stay unruffled and informed him: "I don't want them." "Aye," added John, "don't knock it until you try it." It got a big laugh from everyone, and enlivened an otherwise dull and suspense-free Tribal Council.

Drew saw the whole experience as a valuable and

educational one. "I've learned that I can push myself further than I ever thought I could do. I can go a lot longer without food and I can handle a lot more physically than I ever thought I could. I've learned that I can cope better emotionally in certain situations than I thought I might. I was concerned I might be more up and down and that I might get tearful about stuff. I didn't really. I've missed my family and my boyfriend but I've never felt as if I wanted to go home. You never know how you will cope with the conditions, never having been in a situation like this, with no sleep and no food. I felt we were being tested but it was not as bad as I imagined it would be. As the sort of person who always thinks the worst, it never got that bad. Had it got really bad, that's when I would have wanted to give up and I never did. We were challenged." Drew seems to have forgotten her attempt to force people to vote her off by threatening to sabotage the food.

She also addressed the "Dreary Drew" nickname she acquired among members of the crew. "One of the hardest challenges was coping with the filming, all the cameras in your face, hanging around for things to happen. I knew TV wouldn't be as dynamic as it looks but I never knew it could be as slow as it often can be. If anything was tough, it was coping with that. I thought it would be 24 hours a day but I never thought it could piss you off as much as it sometimes did. I can understand it, but I wasn't expecting it really. Some of the crew were fantastic but there were the odd few who were completely inconsiderate. I'm not sure if they liked me in TV terms; I was miserable to start with, too diplomatic all the way through and I didn't celebrate enough when I won. In general, I haven't been dynamic enough for their tastes. But there's nothing I can do about it. I don't regret the whole experience at all. All in all, if anybody asked me about doing something about this then I would say, 'Absolutely. Go for it.' It's a fantastic opportunity. I totally enjoyed it and it's been brilliant. I am so, so lucky to have got here. It's something I can talk about for the rest of my life and not many others can say that. I feel incredibly fortunate and thankful to Ed Forsdick for giving me this opportunity."

Had Drew really wanted to, given her increased popularity among the male members of South Island, she could have effected a change. She could have targeted John and built on his distrust of Susannah and irritability with Bridget, having already got Jonny on her side. She could have laughed longer and louder at his jokes, a sure-fire way to ingratiate yourself with him. He might not have gone for it but it could have been worth a try. But she was not willing to compromise her morals, even though this had not stopped her threatening sabotage a few days earlier. Drew's ambitions were limited and her attitude became defeatist too quickly. There are ways to advance in *Survivor* without upsetting any moral code; persuasion can be as powerful as coercion. She chose not to go down that route, however. She is aware of her public image and hopes that it will encourage more women to join the fire service.

"I hope it will encourage people to look at firefighting as not just a job for white males. I am on a committee at work to try to encourage more women and people from ethnic minorities to join the fire service. They are completely under-represented. In Oxfordshire, out of 600 fire fighters there are only four women. Hopefully, watching me will have a positive effect. I try to encourage people not to think of firemen, but of firefighters. Dave doesn't agree with me, of course. He's an old-fashioned bloke and not especially keen. He's honest, at least. He's been quite good, not boring me with his time in the service. It's been great meeting Dave, nice to have that sort of connection. I hope that somehow I might have been able to alter his opinion, even if it's just very slightly, about women. Though he'd never bloody admit it."

Back at camp John said she was the first competitor that he felt gutted about when she walked away down the tribal path to oblivion. Both he and Jonny felt guilty. Bridget was unconcerned about all that. Of more interest to her was an incident at Tribal Council, when biting ants attacked her feet and the council was stopped as she was treated. "I've never felt so much pain in such a short period of time," she said. It turns out that a stray peanut had made it on to the floor and was being coveted by the aforementioned ants when Bridget stood on it, causing them to retaliate. Still, it enlivened a pretty dull Tribal Council.

Mad Dogs and Geordies...

The next day's Treemail aroused some interest, indicating as it did that an endurance challenge was next. After the log challenge, people wondered what variation could be found, reasoning that it would not be as arduous since it was only a reward. "Twenty-four hours on a log for a cup of tea and a biscuit," joked John. In fact, in many ways it was harder, as events bore out. In the US version of *Survivor*, there had been a challenge in which the contestants had one hand tied to a barrel above their head, and the barrel was filled with water. They were then left and the last one to remain standing was the winner. In the hot sun, the temptation was to bring the water crashing down on to your head to help cool off. For the British version, it was decided to make things a bit harder. Both hands would be tied above the contestant's heads. This would not allow them to take on water or wipe the sweat off their faces. It was a tough challenge, especially in the midday sun with the temperature climbing well into the nineties Fahrenheit. Because the challenge took place on the beach, a cooling breeze offered some comfort, but it also masked the fierce sun, making contestants feel cooler than they actually were. With this in mind, two medics, Mark Dawes and Andy Thurgood, were on hand if required.

It was obvious that John and Jonny would be favourites. But after his disappointment on the log, Dave was determined to put up a good show. His Immunity Challenge victory had boosted his confidence and he felt good about winning this challenge. "I got a bit confident and I thought, 'I'm gonna push these lads'," he remembers. First to go was Bridget. "I didn't last long and I started to feel faint. As I was coming down, I pulled the rope and took my hands out and I collapsed on the floor." It was only then that she noticed that she had reopened the wound on her knee. It needed re-stitching and this time it took twelve stitches, rather than five.

Next to go was Susannah, whose tonsillitis had kicked in wickedly by this stage. Basically, the last thing she needed to be doing in her condition was standing out to dehydrate in the midday sun. "As soon as I got up on the "Hands Up", my head started going and I couldn't swallow and the sun was beating down and the boys were looking really strong, even Dave – though he was starting to talk to himself just as I was getting down."

This left the three men. John and Jonny were next to each other and started going through their familiar drill of pop trivia. They kept glancing over at Dave, who had closed his eyes in concentration. One of the medics paid him a quick visit and made sure he was OK. John and Jonny kept looking over to see if he was all right and even asked him who was Newcastle United's best player. "Andy Cole," came the weary response. By this time, Dave admits he was losing it somewhat, but pride was forcing him to go on.

"I shut my eyes so I wouldn't get the glare off the sea or the sand. I was at the far end and the other two were at the other end and they could chat but I couldn't hear a word. I got my mind focused. I went through the Newcastle team, the reserve team, the fixtures, then the family. After nearly two hours my breathing was getting quite heavy, and I was bound so my head was down. I couldn't lick my lips or swallow or breathe, so I started breathing through my nose. Apparently Mark came around, enticing people with a meal and I said, 'No'. The other two were still there. A little voice in my head kept saying, 'Keep your hands up'. I was told I was dropping off but a little voice kept telling me to go on. Anyway the medic checked us and said, 'Dave, your heart rate is going up.' I said, 'I'm all right.' " That's the last thing he remembers.

Andy Thurgood was monitoring all the contestants, checking their pulses and watching their respiratory rates. He noticed Dave "go" before the others, showing the early signs of heat stroke. His respiratory rate had risen to 40, from a normal rate of 15–25; he was also becoming quieter, not joining in the banter with the others and he was beginning to focus on just one point on the ground. When Andy went closer he could see signs of distress on Dave's face. Knowing that heat stroke has a 40 per cent mortality rate, he was aware that Dave could not be allowed to continue much longer. After speaking with Ed Forsdick, he went back for another look and the signs were worse.

"It was very serious," Andy says. "I gave him the opportunity to come off himself because by now he was incoherent, his vision was going, his respiratory rate was high and his pulse was weak. He was no longer sweating, which was a very bad sign because it meant his body was no longer able to keep itself cool. In cases of heat stroke the body burns up and the lungs and heart can fail. He had to come down there and then. I tried to untangle his hands and he was reluctant to come down, so I dragged him down and immediately he collapsed and lost consciousness. I then started pouring water everywhere; on his head, on his groin, on his body, which is why you might see me on screen asking for more water. But he was not responding. Then it was a case of "aggressive resuscitation" – cooling, oxygenation and a drip in his arm to get fluids back in to his body as quickly as possible. Within an hour he was sitting up talking, back to normal, though for a few days afterwards he was extremely tired."

Dave blames nobody but himself for what happened. "I was foolhardy and pushed myself too far. But I just wanted to compete against the lads. I got confused and lost my mind a bit because I thought it was an Immunity Challenge, not a Reward. I thought I'd got to win it. I hope they don't show too much of it because my wife will kill us. She told me before I went, 'Don't you try to compete too hard with the young 'uns.' " He is full of praise for the job that the medics did in reviving him so well. When Jonny gave in he still managed to shout from a prone position on the floor, "Well done, Jonny."

As Dave was receiving treatment, the others looked on, horrified. When he finally came round they were mightily relieved. Understandably, after what they had witnessed they were reluctant to push themselves too far. John had believed Jonny would win this, given his reserves of endurance. But the Scotsman suddenly started to feel faint. "The medic came round and asked us questions and you could see Dave wasn't too good. Then Mark came round trying to tempt us with kebabs and Dave never moved. That was better than the actual prize, which was a cooked breakfast. The kebab was far tastier, so I wish I had given in. We started our pop trivia and then we asked Susannah what her favourite sexual position was and

Bridget joined in. It was a good laugh and I felt fine. John said that when Dave went he would go as well, leaving me to win. Then suddenly I went white, my lips went purple and all of a sudden I went deaf. Susannah was asking me questions but I couldn't tell what she was saying. Then I thought I was going to be sick and that I couldn't stand up. I said to John, 'I'm going to go' and he said to wait five minutes. I told Ed to make sure the cameras were on. I can't remember what happened next. Apparently, I fell to my knees. I felt fine before and fully expected to be there until evening. It was heat stroke and dehydration. I just lost too much fluid. I could see what was going on with Dave but did not realise how serious it was until afterwards. After I saw him go I thought there was no point hanging on like he did. Though we did think that the reward might be seeing our relatives, so that's why I wanted to win it and because it was so tough I expected the prize to be amazing, especially after they offered us the kebab. But it was crap."

John did not think so, particularly since it included a made bed. After the challenge, as they all sat sunbathing, he joked about what had happened earlier. "For the next challenge they'll ask us to go to Burma and build a railway. Then they'll bury us up to our necks in sand." So testing was the challenge that the remaining five spent the afternoon sunbathing and recuperating. A cayman had been spotted in the freshwater creek at the back of the camp and plans were set in motion to catch it for sustenance. Up until this point there had been little in the way of needless slaughter to ruffle the feathers of any animal rights activist, lovers of crabs aside, but the contestants were adamant that, given the opportunity, the cayman would be roasting on their fire.

That evening around the fire, the group learned more of Dave's opinion of women firefighters, perhaps speaking more freely now that Drew had gone. He told a story of a London female firefighter who had her period and started crying and so was excused from the watch. The next day, according to Dave, the males started crying to see what the reaction of the station officer was. "I always think the door is there for them to take as much as they can out of the brigade, whether it's sueing for discrimination or things like that. I just think there is more of a chance of them doing something like that than a bloke doing it." John joined in by speaking of his disquiet about proposals for women joining the Marines.

"You've got to walk all night with a heavy pack, dig a trench, have a fire, crawl up to the enemy's trench, jump in with your pickaxe and start battering people with it because you don't want to make any noise. That's the horrible truth about war: it's a horrible thing. Even these days with nuclear war, you are still going to have conflicts with people sneaking up on each other and you've got to have some people you can rely on." John accepted that some women were as barbaric as men, simply that they could not be relied on to be barbaric. Susannah was adamant that exceptional women should be given the chance, both in the Fire Service and the Marines. Dave had a final point to make. "You've got equal opportunities and you've got all these things like a group of women, like the cleaner who's a woman, the cook who's a woman and a clerk who's a woman. They might all be chatting in the kitchen but why can't I go in and say, 'Morning, ladies?' I'm not allowed to call a group of females ladies. We cannot call a manhole a manhole."

His objections then moved on to Helen's language and the severity of her swearing. "I just couldn't believe the language she came out with and apparently her mother is worse!" Susannah agreed, adding that she could picture her on a council estate surrounded by her cousins shouting abuse at a girl across the road. Bridget expressed surprise that someone so intelligent would use such words. This is an example of how Dave and Bridget had many views in common, yet his never seemed to upset the former members of South Island in the same way as Bridget's did.

Dave also revealed that night to camera how he had already made an approach to John and Jonny as a pair. He found they were unshakeable and unbreakable. He admits now that going to them before trying Susannah and Bridget was an error. He does not realise, however, that according to John he was quite close to persuading them to alter their strategy. "Dave came up to me and Jonny and said, 'Look, I don't know how you feel about Susannah but I don't trust her and she doesn't deserve the money. I'd be happy for us to vote them off one by one and then us three be the last three. They're not going to win anything and nor am I.' He put his case well. He said we shouldn't trust Susannah because she was more ambitious than we gave her credit for. He put her down and said 'Keep me. I won't be any threat because I'm not as strong. Once the girls are gone you can get rid of me.' We both thought it was well put but we had made an alliance and a promise and we didn't want to break that. Plus, it could have backfired terribly. Looking back now, though, I wish I had taken him up on it."

That night before going to bed, conversation had turned to how surprised people were that no challenge had yet involved their relatives. All of them had seen the last series where Richard won time with his brother. "There's only eight days or so to go," said Jonny. "They're not going to fly them out with eight days to go." But he was wrong. They had flown them out and on day twenty-eight – Valentine's Day ironically – the five relatives arrived in Bocas. They had arrived in Panama the previous day – together with Drew's boyfriend Robin, who had to be flown out because when the relatives left

London she was still in the game – and spent a relaxing evening in Panama City. The five were Bridget's boyfriend, John, Susannah's husband, Barnaby, Jonny's girlfriend, Ruth, John's girlfriend, Mary and Dave's son, Robert.

As dawn broke, John could not believe how bad a night's sleep he had in the bed. It was too comfortable; he had got used to being cramped. Still, the others coveted his bed, even though he was not too fond of it. As Susannah recollects, for some reason he was very unwilling to let anyone go near it. "Bridget wanted to lie on the bed he had won and he really did not want her to lie on it. He kept going, 'I wouldn't if I were you. You don't know what I've done in it.' He said it wasn't the cleanest bed in the world for some reason. I have no idea what he was on about." If being unable to sleep was bad enough, the breakfast he devoured in seconds reacted badly with his malnourished stomach.

All that was written on the Treemail that morning was five fingerprints, which bamboozled the contestants. They did not realise they were the prints of their nearest and dearest. When they made their way to the Immunity Challenge on Lost Island, with Dave determined to win, they were still clueless as to what would happen next, a fiendish test of memory and, perhaps more importantly, the ability to control their emotions. Ed Forsdick devised the challenge – Family Values – while stationary at a set of traffic lights in London. It was devised to test just how much the contestants would value immunity. The five relatives were sitting at different points on the island. By the side of each was a stack of photos of them. The contestants had to run to each relative in turn, pick up a photo and on the back note their guesses as to who the relatives were, their age, to whom they were related and what that relationship was. The rules were that they were not allowed to touch or speak to their own relative and, if they did, then they would be disqualified. Ed Forsdick fully expected at least one contestant to say "Sod it" and willingly disqualify themselves in favour of contact and a chat. He did not reckon on how focussed they had all become, as Susannah notes. "It did not cross our minds that we could break the rules. By that stage, we were programmed to compete."

There was also an added bonus for the winner, who would get 30 minutes with their loved one as well as the immunity amulet. It was only when Mark said that that they realised what the challenge involved. Until that point they had thought they would just be finding photographs; then the enormity sank in. Everyone went quiet. John was the most surprised at his initial reaction. He had watched *Survivor* the previous year and laughed at the contestants blubbering in front of videos of their families sent from home. "You've only been away for six weeks, you sad idiots," he thought. But when you are hungry, weak, vulnerable and far away from home, it is difficult to control your feelings. Just ask Dave.

No one would describe the Geordie as anything other than a man's man. Yet when he came across his son, he was unable to look him in the eye. "That was the highest and lowest point since I left home. I was a total wreck, a total emotional wreck. It was terrible, bloody terrible. When Mark first explained the game I thought it was a photograph of a loved one at the end of these five paths and you had to look at it and answer the four questions. Then Ed came up and explained the rules, saying you cannot touch and you cannot speak. We were all going, 'What's he on about?' 'What do you mean,' we said. He goes, 'You cannot speak to or touch your relative.' And we looked at each other. 'You mean,' we said, 'we've all got a relative here?' 'Yes,' he goes, 'at the end of each path.' Well, Susannah started bubbling, and I'm getting emotional. I was working out who it would be. I knew it wouldn't be the wife because she doesn't like long-haul flights. I thought it could be Steve because he works in London but then I thought he might find it hard to get off work so I thought it'd be Robert. I thought, 'Bloody hell, I can't handle this.' Sure enough he was there, the third one I saw and I just started blubbering. I lost it. I looked at him and I was crying my bloody eyes out and I was trying to write and of course I got his age wrong. I couldn't say, 'You've bloody upset us, you bugger,' or anything. He was sitting there looking straight ahead and I thought 'You bastard, you've never looked at us once'. But he was upset as well."

Jonny, the eventual winner, saw Ruth and gave her a "cheesy" grin and a "totally naff" thumbs-up. Susannah and Bridget both grinned broadly at their partners, the former blowing a kiss. John was so upset he could not believe it. "I thought, 'I was in the Gulf for four months. I didn't phone anyone then, I don't need to see anyone now.' But when you're caught up in the emotions of it, it's unbelievable. It was great to see her, but really grim because we all felt so low afterwards."

Bridget takes the opposite view: for her it was a very positive experience. "It was so wonderful. After that I could see a picture of John in my mind sitting on the log in Bocas, smiling at me. I found it hard to write his name, or any details down, when I was standing there in front of him. I was the slowest that day. I was walking and taking people's faces in carefully. But when I saw John I just went to pieces, forgot everything, really, my name, his name, his age. It was lovely. I'm glad I didn't win it because half an hour would not have been long enough. I wanted the rest of it. No one spoke on the boat home. I cried all the way back; the tears wouldn't stop. They all only finally stopped when the film crew asked me for the interview and I had tears at the start and by the end they had stopped. Everyone else went off to contemplate. I went 'logging' to take my mind off it. I picked the heaviest bit of wood I could find to deal with it. I am pleased we had that challenge because at home we can talk about it. He came out and saw where we've been doing it, the conditions, the experience and we can talk about it. He got on well with the other partners as well." For her, the whole experience had confirmed that she wanted to spend the rest of her life with John.

Susannah echoes this view. Her main aim was to give Barney the impression that everything was OK and there was no need for him to worry. "I wanted to make it clear I was fine. We just looked for eight seconds, locked eyes and grinned from ear to ear. I went to pieces after seeing Barney. I got Mary and Ruth muddled up. I knew Mary was older than Ruth and I thought Mary looked younger. I also knew Mary looked a bit more bohemian and I knew Ruth had piercing so I thought Mary's braids were bohemian. I also called Bridget's partner John, Les, her ex-husband's name, which I felt really bad about. My brain had gone basically. It had turned to jelly." Later, she joked that she resisted the urge to tell Barney how pasty-faced he was, given that all the contestants now had deep golden tans. "Good job you didn't," joked John, "or it'd be the first divorce of *Survivor*."

At the end of the game, after the results were announced, the contestants were fully expecting that they would be allowed five minutes off camera to say hello to their loved ones. But that was not allowed, much to Dave's chagrin. He let fly a volley of abuse at Ed for being cruel. "Afterwards I said to Ed, 'You could've at least given us five minutes with them off camera. They've come 7,000 miles, man.' The winner still got 30 minutes with the loved one, so what's wrong with just letting us give them a hug and ask if everything's OK? I just walked away – I was fuming and told the cameras to piss off. We went to the take that announced the winner and we all congratulated Jonny. I was pleased for him. The relatives were in a boat in a creek. I just went, 'Hey, Rob' and of course they tried to shut me up and I told them where to go. They were waving and the rest started waving. Mark comes up and he could see we were all emotional. I broke down again and so did John. I shouted to Rob, 'What position is Newcastle in?' And he said, 'Third'. 'What was the score last Saturday?' He says, '3-1.' Then I thought, 'Oh shit, I've forgotten something.' 'How's your Mam?' The camera crew fell about. Three questions and your wife comes last. He shouts back, 'She's fine!' No one else got a word in because I kept shouting all the time. Then it was 'Cut!' I apologised but I wasn't that upset, to be honest."

It was an intensely dramatic moment and an emotional boat ride home for them all. Everyone was silent. Meanwhile, back on Bocas, Jonny and Ruth were reunited for 30 minutes. At first, as he admits, it was awkward because the cameras were there watching, which hardly made for gushing conversation. He also admits Ruth is not the most tactile person in the world. But it was the highlight of the whole experience and gave him strength for the challenges ahead. If they expected her to jump all over him then they were mistaken.

Back at the camp, the question of immunity was forgotten as everyone tried to take in what had happened. When Jonny returned, bearing the uplifting news from home that Princess Margaret had died, he found everyone introverted and morose. He apologised for celebrating too excessively. Stephen Flett, the psychologist, made a trip to the island to check that everyone was feeling mentally sound and there would be no suicides. There were moments of humour. Jonny recalled how Barney smiled warmly at him. "I'd take that as a green light," said John. "He's a very generous man," joked Susannah. But within minutes the game was back on, as normal. A huddled chat took place between Susannah, John and Jonny. "Bridget cannot win immunity next time," she hissed. "She cannot. She cannot. I'd think I'd rather die," she added, which seemed something of an overstatement.

As if reflecting everyone's mood, the rain poured down that night, getting in the shelter and soaking everyone's clothes. Apart from Bridget, few could sleep, a result of the weather and the turbulent emotions that the day had stirred. People's minds had turned towards home and the people there. But first there were some very important challenges to compete in and some very important decisions to consider. This was no time for self-pity.

Week 5

North/South Divide

On the morning of day twenty-nine, Dave, who had resigned himself to going, decided that he would make one last effort to try to persuade Susannah and Bridget to join him in an alliance against John and Jonny. But Susannah, whose tonsillitis was at its worst, saw herself in an alliance with Jonny and John, not one with Bridget, though she admits that it crossed her mind to turn the game on its head and team up with Dave. But for Susannah, remaining true to her word had become more important than winning. It seemed as if her whole purpose for being there, which was to win, had changed. Her ambition was now to make amends for what she did to Lee.

"It crossed my mind to break the alliance and go with Dave and Bridget, of course it did. Bridget never wanted to play the game; she wanted the friendships. It became clear that it was quite possible that, if John won the immunity, he would take Jonny through. I did not try to strike a deal with John because I had my deal with Jonny and I wanted to stay true to that. After the Lee thing, I wanted to stick to my promises. We had been through a lot by that point. I decided to stick with that alliance even though strategically it could have been better to split off and go with Dave and Bridget. But there were cons to that strategy as well. It could have happened that in the final three Dave and Bridget could have won immunity and voted me off. I would prefer John or Jonny winning a million pounds to Dave or Bridget – that's just a personal thing. Also, they were more deserving, I thought. I would have no guarantee that those two would stick with me as much as John or Jonny would. But the main thing was that I had done a deal with John and Jonny and an internal agreement with Jonny the next day. We had stayed together a long time."

There was also the fact that Bridget was increasingly irritating her. Susannah's frustration stemmed from Bridget's domination of the fire, which she claimed was partly show for the camera to prove how able and active she was. "I would love to kill the chicken," she told the camera, "and I really love cooking and when I have the chance I enjoy it. However, that is taken away from us so much that it is starting to get people's backs up and so people shut down instead of trying to compete." She had noticed as well that Bridget was becoming increasingly confident, arrogant almost, now that the demise of the former North Island was strengthening her position. Some of this can be put down to Susannah's tonsillitis, which was making her lacklustre, while Bridget by contrast was bursting with energy. But Bridget had every right to be confident. She had done far better than she had imagined and once Dave was gone she would set her mind on trying to win immunity. It never occurred to her to side with Dave, or not until he approached her and Susannah at the creek.

"It didn't cross my mind to pair with Dave, but then I don't think Susannah would have budged. In all honesty, it would have been a waste of time. Dave approached me and asked if we were voting as a tribe that night and we said yes. Had he been a bit more forceful then maybe I would have listened, but he wasn't. I'm not a political person, those sort of things never bothered me. I was interested in just getting as far as I could by trying hard around the camp and doing well in the challenges. Never at any stage did I think I would win. The million pounds seemed miles and miles away."

Dave's recollection is that he put his argument more forcefully than that. In his version, he told them that they had little chance of defeating the two other men and that if they wanted to have any chance of the million then they should form an alliance with him. "I tried to split the two lasses by telling them that the lads were the strongest and they would get rid of the girls when they wanted. But they couldn't see that. I told them they were merely prolonging their agony, because the rice was getting low and everyone was really, really hungry. I said, 'You won't reach the final. They'll vote you off.' They said they had made a promise but I told them we were one tribe and they should start thinking for themselves. I said, 'Look, there's a million pounds at stake. Never mind promises, they're out of the window.' I couldn't get that across to them, I honestly couldn't. John and Jonny had an agreement, and a strong one. But the lasses couldn't see they were going to get stung."

There is some merit in Dave's argument. Given her lack of popularity, though she had everyone's respect, the only way Susannah could have won a majority on the jury was by taking Bridget through with her to the last two. To do that, she needed to ally herself with Dave and Bridget that night and get rid of John on one of the rare occasions when he did not have immunity. She might not have earned everyone's affection on the jury, but she had their respect. It would have earned the ire of Jonny, but he would not have been surprised. Life would have been difficult around the camp for a few days but that would be a small price to pay for a million pounds. Jonny may have tried to stage an alliance with Dave, but Dave would have been daft to switch allegiance. Against either Bridget or Susannah he would have been a sure thing. In fact, he would have been against anybody. Jonny would have gone next had he not won immunity and then Susannah could have hoped to win the final Immunity Challenge and vote off Dave. Susannah did not take this path because she had become friends with Jonny and, to a lesser extent, John and she did not want to break her word. Tellingly, before Tribal Council, John admitted: "There's no need for Susannah and Bridget to vote tribally. It's not in their self-interest. We've brainwashed them." This was said only half in jest.

Jonny and John, in particular, saw Susannah, despite her harsh words about the shepherdess earlier in the day, spend a lot of time with Bridget, whispering. They were certain Dave would make an approach. John became convinced he was being voted off. "I was convinced that Susannah and Bridget and Dave had struck a deal before we went to Tribal Council, because there was loads of whispering going on. You didn't want to leave any of them, particularly Dave, in case he used his Geordie charm. He had approached us to begin with and that made Jonny and me live to it. He should have gone straight to Bridget and Susannah. It would have perhaps made sense, with hindsight, for us to have got rid of Susannah and taken Dave through with us because he might not have done so well at that last Immunity Challenge, "Time's Up". But we were worried about Susannah because she was like a floating voter and had the potential to wreck things for us. We asked her if she was still going to vote for Dave that night and she said, 'Yes' and we were both staring at her intently, watching her body language, to see if she was lying. I genuinely thought I might go that night because Jonny had immunity."

Ironically, Jonny became more and more annoyed as the day wore on that Dave was going and not Bridget. He would say after Tribal Council that he hated making promises like the one he made to Bridget. But John was on hand to convince him that keeping Dave would be foolish. He pointed out how, on last year's *Survivor*, Charlotte was not voted off as the tribe turned on each other and she sneaked through to win. Now Dave is about as different from Charlotte as it is possible to be, but John was adamant that the same should not be allowed to happen. Dave was a serious threat to both of them if he won immunity and made the final two, whereas both had extremely good chances of garnering more votes than Susannah or Bridget from the jury. Reluctantly, Jonny agreed and he made sure that Susannah was not going to break the agreement either. She agreed she would not. So, that evening at Tribal Council, Dave left, leaving behind some memorable moments. One crew member joked that at the end of *Survivor*, Dave would be voted Prime Minister, given how popular he was on the island and how popular he would be with the public. He had shown bravery, determination and unfailing humour, in even the blackest circumstances. He may not have been the most outgoing or extroverted of the group, or the biggest show-off. He was, however, decent, honest and modest: a true gentleman, even considering his rather old-fashioned views on "ladies".

John offered this tribute to the camera on the day he voted Dave off. "It is a complete travesty because Dave is such a nice bloke. He played the game with incredible spirit. You just had to watch him in the last Reward Challenge when he was drifting in and out of consciousness and still keeping his arms up in the end. He had to be manhandled off the game because he would have been there until he died. He just looked so ill but there were no signs of him giving up. It is a tragedy that he goes before Bridget." Tragedy is not the word and John is wrong: Bridget deserved to get where she did. But he was also right in that Dave's courage won everyone's respect – though his wife, Rita, might not agree.

Bizarrely, Bridget had asked that Dave vote for her to even up the votes, putting her and Susannah on five apiece. Neither of the two boys had any votes against them. In her words it made things "equal". Turkeys do vote for Christmas, it seems.

In his interview with Mark, Dave spoke of how friendly the experience had been and his surprise at being selected for the programme. Later, interviewed for this book, he went in to more detail about the whole bewildering experience. "To be truthful, when I applied, I thought my age would go against us. I decided to give it a go because if you don't try then you don't get. I was dead chuffed when I got the reply for the first interview. Funnily enough, my wife had had a dream that if I passed the first interview then I'd be there. I told her not to be silly. I was just privileged to get past the first one. I like things like this because it taxes the mind. I've only had two jobs: the Royal Navy and the Fire Service. They were both challenging in themselves but this would be the ultimate challenge and I wanted to see if I could do it. And I could.

"We went to Panama and arrived under false names. At the airport, this massive four by four arrived to pick me up. I was thinking, 'This must have cost a fortune.' This had never happened to me in my life before, being ferried about, picked up, everything arranged for you, best hotels. It's all been a bit, 'Bloody hell, what's happenin' here?' I always knew it would be exciting and every second something new was happening to me that I'd never experienced before and it was really smashing. I got to the Holiday Inn and I opened the door and there was the biggest bed I had ever seen in my life, king-size. There was furniture and all this and I thought, 'This'll do, like.' I opened the minibar and it was empty and I thought, 'That's a good thing. No temptation.' We were there for two nights and we were there all next day and we couldn't leave. It wasn't too bad. I know some of the others found the porn on the TV but I'm past all that. I found the football instead."

He actively embraced the whole experience and savoured every second. Even on the jury, he enjoyed himself as best he could, sipping beer on the beach with his old tribe, parading around the lodge balcony with Alastair in matching pink towels, piling back on the weight he had lost. But when it came to devising questions for the final two, he took that responsibility as seriously as possible, realising that the decision would completely alter the winner's life. It could not have happened to a nicer man. Perhaps, for *Survivor*, he was too nice. Good guys, after all, rarely come first.

The next morning, day thirty, it was obvious that Bridget would have to win the next Immunity Challenge to have the slightest hope of remaining on the island. Realising this, John and the other two were desperate to win immunity to avoid having one of them go. John was still sticking to his agreement with Jonny, even though he admitted that could cost him a chance of winning the million.

"It is funny," he told the camera, "if someone had explained my tactics to me at the start of the game, then I wouldn't have believed that I would jeopardise such a significant amount of money just for some contract written in the sand four weeks ago with someone I had only met 48 hours previously. But it is how you want to be perceived and how you feel you have played the game. I was lucky enough to be in Australia four years ago and I saw the first American series of *Survivor* and how the eventual winner, Richard Hatch, seemed to play the game. He is now a buzzword for dishonesty and disloyalty, somebody who will do anything. OK, he is probably living in a penthouse on Fifth Avenue but that aside, he came across really badly and you will be remembered for that. It is just something I don't want to be remembered for. It probably sounds very moralistic but I would rather be loyal to the alliance I made at the start and stick with it, whatever the outcome. I don't think I made too many mistakes tactically, though I have made a bit of a dick of myself on several occasions."

This idea of a moral code seemed to spread through all the contestants, as if by osmosis. Everyone caught the moral contagion, as if anyone who stepped outside the bounds of accepted behaviour would have been lynched, or at the very least ostracised. Everyone had come to the opinion that a good reputation was worth more than a million pounds – though both, of course, would be ideal. The commandment was laid down: 'Thou shalt not stitch up thy neighbour nor break an alliance." No one had the courage, or the greed, to break it. John also maintained that he was never that worried about Dave forming an alliance with Susannah, even though it was something he had admitted to earlier. He felt the class difference was gaping. "Sitting around the camp fire last night, Dave said how much he liked liver and bacon and Susannah said, 'Yes, I love it as well, thinly sliced in a warm tossed salad' and Dave just had this look on his face. I mean, Dave doesn't want to know what full-bodied red wine goes with a bacon buttie, so perhaps Susannah has shown a lack of judgement. She has sometimes alienated the other people because she hasn't realised the sort of people she is talking to, people like Dave and Drew."

Despite the four former South Island members now being on their own again, and being given a new smaller boat with which to fish, now Columbus tribe had been halved, the feeling was very different from those halcyon earlier days. The game had changed a great deal and people's energy levels were lower, and friendships were at a very different stage. The light-hearted attitude before merger had given way to a more serious outlook. In particular, people had grown fed-up with Bridget. This is no slur on Bridget, she was just being herself, but it is a long time to be in close proximity to someone with whom you would not naturally choose to spend a significant period of time. As Jonny admits, "If I spend two weeks on holiday with my girlfriend, I need time to myself." He dismisses accusations that he was two-faced in giving Bridget the impression that he liked her a great deal while slagging her off in private and to the camera. "Bridget had been with us from day one, so while the merger was good because we met the others and heard new stories, lots of them from Alastair, I'd just had enough of Bridget. People can say what they want about me being two-faced about Bridget, but it was only five and a half weeks and it was not as if I was having to work with her long-term. If she was a colleague at work then I may have learnt to bite my tongue and get on with it, but that wasn't the case. I disagreed with some of the things she said and some of her views."

That morning was the weight-guessing Reward Challenge. Each contestant had been weighed at the airport in Bocas on arrival. Now, in turn, after examining themselves in the mirror, the remaining four had to guess how much weight they had lost. They were then weighed on the same scales that they had used at the airport to see how close their estimates were. Whoever guessed nearest to the true amount would win. John, Jonny and Susannah all guessed their weight loss within two kilos. Jonny had lost most, well over a stone and a half. Interestingly, all four believed that they had lost more weight than the scales indicated and have a theory to support that view. In their hotels the day before the game started each of them had used their hotel scales to record their weight. The next day at the airport, when they stood on the scales, all four were miraculously and exactly three kilos lighter. Either their hotel scales or the airport scales were incorrect. The debate rages on … but ultimately, it made no difference.

Later that morning, Mark arrived with their prizes: care packages brought by their relatives from home. Barney hardly helped Susannah dispel her air of middle-class affluence by including chorizo sausage, parmesan cheese and red wine. But then John, who as a barrister is hardly forced to exist on double egg and chips every night, also received wine and cashew nuts from Mary. All it needed was for Jonny to produce a Demis Roussos CD from the selection Ruth had given him and a few Wagon Wheels and it would have been a re-creation of *Abigail's Party*. Susannah's book, the Brazilian writer Paolo Coelho's new age bestseller *The Alchemist*, did not go down too well with the others. It was described by one acerbic reviewer as "simplistic, repetitious, sanctimonious claptrap, it's only saving grace is its short length". By the end of her reading, the boys were screaming for more Shakespeare.

Bridget could not hide her disappointment at having been left out of this gift-giving, which was widely accepted as the best reward yet. She had to remove herself, wondering wistfully about what John had put in her pack. As the boys spoke callously of giving her an empty bottle of wine, Susannah decided she would share, giving her some chocolate.

Jonny reluctantly offered up some raisins as well. Watching this, it was difficult not to feel for Bridget. She felt that she had made genuine friends in Susannah, Jonny and John and was oblivious to their crueller comments. She had been nothing but herself, despite Drew's rather odd assertion that she was false. She did not try to hide her views, objectionable as many found them, and felt no need to apologise for them. While some of John and Jonny's frustration was understandable – Bridget might have been too much and some of her stories did go on without either a point or an end, but then that was a criticism also levelled at Alastair – some of their comments were completely unjustified. Shame on you lads. At least John admits to feeling guilty about it, which is more than can be said for Jonny.

"She's a sound person and she's quite funny," says John. "I just got fed up with this maternal thing she had going on and she was very protective of it. Like cooking the rice. She was always fussing around you. She told these really long stories as well. Alastair was a bit like that, constantly interrupting himself whenever he started a yarn. 'There was this girl called Jane King, right … no, no … it was Jane, Jane McAllister, aye, that was it … and her brother was called John, that's the one, John McAllister, married a Swedish woman … or was she Irish … no, he's a single feller. He might be gay.' They went on and on like that. But they could be quite funny and interesting, occasionally at least, but Bridget had lived a sheltered life and her stories weren't quite as interesting. I feel guilty about slagging her off but when I was there it affected me. But I hope she doesn't take it too much to heart, I really do."

In Bridget's view all was rosy in the garden. She was desperately disappointed not to have got her package from her boyfriend John, not because of the food or drink that might have been in it, but for the personal effects it might have contained, like a picture of her two daughters. Her daughters were from a previous marriage. She and John had first met and gone out together when they were 15 and though they split up they had always kept in touch. When John's marriage ended, they got back together. Their families know each other, and their children are friends. She describes him as her "best mate".

But she also believed she had "best mates" for life in Jonny, Susannah and John. In an interview on day thirty she spoke of how she did not see the four of them as an alliance, but as a "friendship". In the spirit of that friendship she told them, so she claimed, that if she did not win the next Immunity Challenge then they should vote her off. "They were quite shocked that I did that but I want to remain close to them," she told the camera. "I don't want there to be a battle, so I would rather one of them should win it and we should still remain friends. I just think that's me; I tend to put other people first before myself. I know this is a game but the friendships we have made between the four of us are so very real that I want them to continue long after this is filmed and has been on the TV, even ten years down the line. I still want this friendship so I won't sacrifice anything else. I'd rather have the friendship than the million pounds, definitely."

Returning to why she asked to be voted off, she added: "I don't want to be sitting here thinking, 'Are they going to vote me off or aren't they?' If I tell them to vote me off then I can enjoy the rest of my time here without thinking about it all the time." She said she was dreading the jury because she would be the only person from South Island and feared she would be ostracised because North Island had taken the game so seriously, while she had treated it like a holiday. Asked who she wanted to see win the million, she said Jonny and Susannah. But while she accepted that she would go if she did not win immunity, she had no intention of going down without a fight. She would give her all to the next challenge.

That day's Treemail had read:

When the sun goes down tonight
A Challenge will begin.
Pack your bags for a night away
There's immunity to win

The island will be empty
The landscape will be stark,
And when night falls we'll see who's brave
And who's scared of the dark.

That evening the four of them were taken to a small mangrove island and placed at four different points at its extremity, with a bowl of rice, a banana, a hurricane lamp and a cameraman. At each station was an envelope, which they could not open until a flare was fired, at which point the challenge started. It gave them a bearing towards the centre of the island, which they had to find, with the first person getting there winning immunity. The catch was that no one knew when the flare would be fired. As night fell they paced around waiting for the signal. As the darkness descended, some guessed that they would be left until morning, but others didn't. Jonny stayed up all night, thinking the flare could go off at any time, not realising, as the other three had, that to send people careering through razor-sharp thickets in pitch darkness would have been a bit too dangerous. All of them were bitten to pieces by mites.

The person who experienced the most discomfort was John. Earlier that day the tribe had gone out fishing and he had borrowed the snorkel and mask from Susannah. Even though it would break several rules of medicine, he claimed that as soon as he returned his throat started to ache and he began to feel ill. By evening he was feeling thoroughly rotten. He had caught Susannah's tonsillitis. It did not affect him, however, the next morning at 8am, 14 hours after they were dropped off, when the signal for the game to start was finally fired. He took his bearing, left his instructions and made straight for the centre of the island, taking the most direct route. He walked through thick branches and hedges, cutting his leg badly, but did not falter. Hash, the security guard and former US Navy SEAL, after surveying the island, estimated that the winning time would be around 30 minutes, given the density of the jungle. Little John managed it in seven minutes, startling all the crew and Mark when he burst from the undergrowth. Since the others were nowhere to be seen, Mark handed John the amulet and left him alone there to be found by them.

They were having increasing difficulty finding their way. Susannah had practised with a compass before leaving England but it did her no good whatsoever. "Jonny and I were crap. I knew what I should be doing because I had practised orienteering on Dartmoor. I knew I had to take a bearing but I could not see anything above the jungle canopy so I had to stop every ten metres. I was obviously way off. Then I bumped into Jonny and our bearings took us to the sea. Then we found John's camp and we read his bearing so we followed his bearing from that point. Then we met up with Bridget and she crashed through just before us." Both she and Jonny knew John had won at that point and they were safe. Bridget was not so sanguine. As she crashed through the thicket, falling head first in front of John she snarled, "You bastard!" which startled the diminutive Ulsterman. "A tough cookie" is how many people describe Bridget, and she had been totally committed to winning the challenge. She did not realise how close she was.

At one point she passed within ten yards of the centre point, but did not realise it.

It is during this game that John believes he missed his chance to get rid of Susannah and thereby markedly improve his chances of reaching the final. With the benefit of hindsight he realised he could have found the centre of the island and then retreated and hid until Bridget broke through the undergrowth and won immunity. He and Jonny would then, he claims, have voted for Susannah and because she had so many votes against her she would have been voted off. But that was a plan he devised in his kitchen in Winchester; he would have done better to consider it in a jungle in Panama.

Back at camp, John explained how after the challenge he had been approached by Jonny to make sure their alliance was still strong. "It's odd because I think that even he is getting a little bit jittery and there is always an element of doubt and I just reassure him every time. I don't need reassurance from him because I trust him and, if he did change his mind, there is nothing I could do because it would be done on the night of Tribal Council. It's one of those things that I don't feel worried about. If I go, I go, and if he holds his word, brilliant." On the subject of Bridget, he admired her attitude in the challenge, which evidenced how much she still wanted to win, despite her talk of a "holiday". "I think the All Blacks front row would have had trouble stopping her this morning. She is a woman of two personalities, I think: what she says on camera and what she's like around the camp. From what we see in camp, she's a single-minded and unusual person." He then retold the oft-related story of Bridget's ignorance of September 11. She was different, that's for sure, but in *Survivor 2* difference was seen as bad, not something to be celebrated.

Later as he and Jonny walked to the freshwater creek John spoke of his deep-rooted wish to beat Susannah, "because I deserve to". Jonny also cast doubt about Bridget's holiday. "I don't think she wants to go at all," he told the camera. "I think she came here looking to win the million. I think she was quite ambitious about it but I think that was part of the way she played it, to pretend she was the mother figure. She certainly wanted to be there at the end. She's lovely, it's just sometimes that she's so boring … and she's not as caring or as loving as she might make herself appear." A similar argument could be targeted at Jonny for the way he managed to ingratiate himself with everyone, while being able to share caustic remarks and observations about them with John.

That night they all sat around the fire and talked about the emotional side of the game. Bridget said she had coped better than she imagined she would, especially being apart from her daughters. "I think you just shut down," Susannah added, "You just focus and eliminate the part of your life that is not relevant." John's theory was that the experience had toughened them up, mentally and physically. He had cried twice though: the first time when he was set off by Dave, so he claimed, after the "Family Values" challenge and the second time the day before when he got a picture of his father in his care package. "I don't think you are a total poof, mate," Jonny told him reassuringly.

They were not the only ones whose emotions were running high. On the jury, Drew's realisation that Robin had been flown out to Panama with the rest of the relatives boiled over into frustration and anger. She had first scented something suspicious when she was handed a Valentine's Card from Robin, which, or so she was told, had been mailed to the crew's hotel in Bocas, when in reality it had been brought from England. Then, when she attended the Tribal Council that saw Dave voted off and heard Mark question the others about the challenge, she twigged. Working back, she managed to deduce that Robin must have left England with the others, given it took more than a day to reach Bocas from London. She was still in the game when the relatives left London so Robin must have been with them. She slept on that thought and then the next day confronted Kevin Reid, who chaperoned the contestants when they were not involved in the game, demanding to see Robin.

"I was very upset," she said afterwards, "because Robin had flown out expecting at least to see me. I am a suspicious person I suppose, and I knew something was up when I got the Valentine's Card. I just wanted to see him because all the others got to see their relatives, even if they didn't get to speak to them. Instead, Robin flew all that way for nothing really. The more I thought about it the more pissed off I got. I just really wanted to see him. I wasn't in the game any more so I felt the rules should not apply to me and that I should be allowed to see him for ten minutes at least."

Kevin tried to reason with her. In Bocas he had already explained to Robin that Drew had been voted off and therefore he would not see her. He was hardly jumping with joy at the news but he accepted the rules of the game and consoled himself by joining in the mammoth drinking spree the six relatives undertook, both in Panama City, then in Bocas and then the following night in Panama City once more. Drew would have none of Kevin's explanations, however, and demanded to see her boyfriend. In an uncanny echo of her behaviour on the island when she threatened to destroy food and not help around camp unless she was voted off, she threatened not to allow herself to be filmed while on the jury or carry out any other tasks expected of her unless she was allowed to see Robin before he returned to England. She even offered to pay for herself to fly to Panama City to meet him. While the other jury members thought her behaviour over the top, Kevin informed Ed Forsdick and they decided to try and arrange the meeting rather than risk Drew walking off the show, even though if she did that then she would be in breach of her contract.

First of all they attempted to book a seat for her on a flight to Panama City the next morning but all flights were fully booked. Planet 24 then looked in to chartering a plane for her but while a plane could be found in such short time, no fuel could. Drew would have to settle for a phone call to Robin's hotel room. Still somewhat groggy after several nights of revelry with the others, he eventually answered the phone and the pair had their conversation. Drew accepted that every effort had been made at her behest and agreed to follow the rules from that point on, though it hardly helped her relations with the production company. It was not the first time she had been the source of trouble – after the deep-sea fishing trip it was discovered she had helped herself to a packed lunch that belonged to an Argentinean cameraman, who was off somewhere being seasick, so it could be argued he did not need it. It seems a pointless thing to have done though when she and Jonny were catching fish to feast on later and were being supplied with a steady stream of alcohol. When Ed Forsdick found out it was too late to disqualify her, but the fact was that she was next to be voted off anyway. It was this light-fingered piece of larceny that led Jonny to refer to her as 'Fagin' during the final Tribal Council.

The next day was Bridget's last, and she took time to enjoy it as best she could. Its highlight was the capture of the cayman in the creek, causing much delight for everyone, the cayman apart. Its existence had been debated for days. It had first been spotted by a camera crew, and then it was sighted by the tribe. They set traps but failed to catch it, until this day when, not the large cayman, but one off its offspring was unfortunate enough to become entangled in the fishing net. There was not even the slightest hesitation over whether to kill it or not: these people were hungry and they were determined to eat to keep up their strength. Checks were made about whether it was a protected species and, since it wasn't, it was fair game. It endured a gruesome death, having a knife plunged into its brain before its head was severed. Wimpishly, Jonny and John then bowed out while Susannah set about the poor creature with a relish that would have shamed Norman Bates. She gutted it, an experience that she said she would never forget – a feeling shared by the cameramen who filmed it in all its technicolor glory. As a result, there was a new supper that evening before they left for Tribal Council and – surprise, surprise – it tasted like chicken.

That evening, Bridget was voted off as expected. Because neither of the boys had a vote against them, and she did not want to spoil that clean sheet, and Susannah already had five votes, she decided to vote for Susannah on the basis that one more vote would not hurt her. In her interview with Mark she hinted that she knew that Susannah would vote for Jonny but would not confirm it. She also confessed that prior to the game she was worried about how she would mix with people, as she spends most of her time with sheep. The theory that she was unworldly and had only experienced limited travel was blown away when she revealed that she had been skiing three times, and had taken a luxury trip to Antigua, a break in Amsterdam and a shopping trip to New York. So much for the poverty-stricken farmer having to exist on £60 a week. Asked whether she believed herself to be a "successful country bumpkin among city slickers", she agreed. "I wouldn't say they did not have a clue, because they did have some idea. But they never put it into practice."

She spoke of the three people left on the island. "Jonny is

a very loveable guy. He is one of the nicest men I have met for a very long time. He is so genuine it is unbelievable .... John is Mr Chimp, Mr Athletic, Mr Agility, Mr Everything, I mean he just goes and wins everything and makes a fool of himself. I think he is very materialistic – a nice guy, but his sights are set much higher than a lot of people's. Susannah is lovely. If I was her Mum I would be so proud of her. We are quite different and that is probably why I think an awful lot of her. Susannah could be one of my friends for the rest of my life, definitely. I have learnt so much from her, she is so intelligent and so clever … she has been there for me, a shoulder to cry on when things haven't been good for me. She is lovely."

As she delivered these eulogies, the remaining three arrived back at their camp and, as if they knew what Bridget was saying about them, some were already feeling guilty about what they had said in the voting booth, particularly Jonny. "I think I was a bit nasty in my speech," he admitted. But as they went to bed they were all looking forward to waking up the next morning and not having Bridget fussing over the fire, making them feel guilty about not getting up at the crack of dawn.

Bridget would also be lying in, or at least trying to, after a night in a bed with clean sheets. Looking back, she remembers the experience fondly and hopefully it won't be spoiled when she sees some of the more candid comments made on camera by Jonny, John and Susannah. She should remember that it is not a natural amount of time to spend with strangers, with whom you have little in common, and that petty irritations will emerge. All three stress how much they liked Bridget but just struggled to cope with certain aspects of her personality. She is glad that everyone, contestants, crew and the public got to see all sides of her personality, including her short temper. Getting to the last four exceeded her expectations and she is rightly proud that she defeated Drew in the Oxfordshire battle between firefighter and farmer. In fact, she is proud of the whole of her performance and is rueful only about her failure to win a challenge, which would have set the seal on her whole experience.

"I was relaxed and at ease with myself and pleased I did a good job. I was as nice as I could be without being sickly. Yes, there are some of these people I will never see again, but then I don't want to. I had a good time with no regrets at all. I will also have a scar on my knee that will forever remind me of the time I was in *Survivor*."

The name's Bond: Unbreakable Bond

Susannah believed that she was an equal part of the alliance she had formed with Jonny and John. She wasn't. Both John and Jonny were adamant that they would take each other through if they won immunity, even when both reckoned they had a better chance of winning the ultimate prize if they took Susannah through to the final two. When asked by Mark if their bond was unbreakable, John said emphatically that it was. Jonny never said so publicly, for fear, presumably of upsetting Susannah, with whom he had a secret agreement that John did not know about. On the boat back from Tribal Council, Jonny had whispered to John an apology for not saying their bond was unbreakable, reassuring him that the bond was still strong. Unfortunately, as John points out, Jonny is the "most unsubtle man on the planet", whose whispers can be heard for miles around and he was worried that Susannah might have heard. If she did, she let nothing slip.

The threesome formed within the first week of *Survivor* had seen them through to the last week. Neither of them were certain how it would play out from here on. Jonny was 95 per cent certain that John would take him through but was not sure about Susannah. Susannah felt she would be taken through by either, given her comparative lack of popularity with the jury, but also believed that Jonny would be true to his word and would take her through, should he gain immunity. The person who felt the most confident was John, who trusted Jonny to take him through and felt that Susannah would also, given that she would have a better chance with the jury against him rather than Jonny. In quieter moments, which became increasingly frequent as tonsillitis set in and his hungry body fought the disease, John admits to allowing himself to be cocky about his chances of making the final two.

What was at the forefront of their minds on day thirty-three was the nature of the following day's Immunity Challenge. The boys were hoping that it would be something physical, or a test of endurance. Susannah wanted a swimming challenge, believing herself the strongest swimmer of the three, though Jonny thought that John was the better swimmer. This debate took up many hours around the camp until all three realised that it was pointless agonising over something that was out of their control. Instead, they enjoyed lazing around the camp, Bridget's dominance of the fire a distant memory.

First, they had a Reward Challenge. This was "Fallen Comrades", which will be known to fans of *Survivor 1* as the "girly" challenge that ended Richard the psychiatrist's cloying and arrogant belief that he was destined to win *Survivor*. Here it was the route to either a pizza or a phone-call home. One thing had not changed, however, and that was that it proved women are better at retaining personal information than men are. These were the questions in full:

1. **Q:** What rewards did North Tribe win after Canoe Rescue?

A: Tin of pork and beans, tin of fruit, shampoo, razor, bucket, toothbrush, chocolate, biscuits, cooking wok.

Susannah right.

2. Q: How many spiders were caught in total at the cave?

A: 29

Nobody right.

3. Q: What was the name of the tree from which your bows were carved in "Ever Decreasing Targets"?

A: Pifar

Susannah right.

4. Q: Which member of the jury is a qualified scuba diving instructor?

A: Helen

Susannah, Jonny, John right.

5. Q: In a dramatic moment in "Family Values", Dave called out to his son and asked him what the score was in Newcastle United's last game. What was that score?

A: 3-1

John right.

6. Q: Drew's luxury item was a photo of her boyfriend. Who else was in the picture, and what is their name?

A: Her dog, Bess

Nobody right.

7. *Q:* What star sign is Alastair?

    A: Aries

Susannah right.

8. *Q:* During the Log Stand, how many meals did Mark eat with the survivors?

    A: 5

Susannah, John, Jonny right.

Susannah won and was given the chance of a phone call to Barney or a pizza, fries, a drink and chocolate cake to be delivered by the fictional "Popa's Pizza". To many people's surprise, Susannah elected for the phone call. She tried their home phone number and there was no response. Then she tried Barney at work and the phone rang and rang, prompting her to wonder out loud where he was. "At Spearmint Rhino's," joked John, whose humour betrayed how gaunt and weak he was looking as a result of his illness. Finally, Barney picked up the phone and Susannah had her five-minute chat.

"Five days previously at the Family Values challenge, I had seen him and not been able to speak to him. I don't know what he was thinking," she says, explaining why she turned down the food. "Afterwards, they were led past us and we were blindfolded so we couldn't see them. I put my thumbs down to let him know that I hadn't won. Then I was worried in case he thought that I was miserable and unhappy and I was really worried about him. I just wanted to speak to him because I was missing him. I did not realise he had been boozing it up in Bocas with all the others. He was so delighted to speak to me that it didn't matter that it was in front of 40 cameras. But I dreamt about pizza that night, I must admit."

Back at the camp she was teased, something that was becoming sport for John and Jonny, though Susannah took it in good heart, often giving as good as she got. In reality, the others were quite happy they did not win: John because he knew the pizza would play as much havoc with his bowels as the cooked breakfast had and that if he had phoned Mary he would have been a "blubbing mess". Jonny had also seen Ruth recently and spent time with her so his need for contact was not so great. "I wasn't too bothered," he told the camera.

That night around the fire there were few signs of unease among the group. They were all talking about what they would do when they got home. John was looking forward to a round of golf, a few beers with his mates and a game of tennis "down the club". Susannah said she would meet Barney and perform "marital duties" ("What, you'd do the washing straight away?" joked John) and then go out for a meal after a bath and a bottle of wine. The next morning, she would buy five newspapers from Tesco, a bottle of Orange and Raspberry crush, an almond croissant and a fresh fruit salad. Jonny was interested only in beer, Ruth and McDonald's. In fact the only worry that seemed to cross their minds that evening was the impression they would make on television. Jonny got the vapours about his and John's antics with the home video camera. "I really hope that it's obvious to everyone that everything John and I have said has been totally tongue-in-cheek!" It was a bit late for that

When they woke up the challenge was on everyone's mind. The Treemail indicated that it would have something to do with time but they did not know what. The first shock they got was arriving back on South Island, where the challenge would be held, for the first time since they had left it at merger, almost three weeks previously. As they arrived, they sat down on logs while Mark explained the rules to them. They had to estimate when an hour had elapsed and the second they thought it had, they were to light their torch and stand outside the circle. Immediately after the rules were explained, in particular that they could not use the ground on which to count, they were taken to three separate points while Ed Forsdick went to each to make sure they were certain about the rules. This would also prevent any collaboration, a thought that had gone through John's mind. "There was a really easy way to win that last Immunity Challenge. I was dying to talk to Jonny because I knew he would not have clicked the easiest way to do it. As soon as Mark explained it, I thought 'This is easy.' Basically, I don't bother counting, I just watch Susannah and as soon as she moves I beat her to it. Then when she got up Jonny should have got up straight after her and, as long as she isn't bang on, we would have won. That's why Ed split us up. It made perfect sense. I was staring at Jonny thinking he will click on to it but he just sat there like Kermit on a log, hand on his pulse. His bloody pulse – I don't believe it."

But that was not Jonny's first thought. "As soon as Mark explained the rules I thought, 'Susannah's going to win this'. I looked at John but I had no chance to catch his eye to say, 'This is not what we wanted'."

There was time for each to devise their method of counting. John knew his immediately, having recalled the film *Good Will Hunting* in which a character counts an hour by twitching his thumb. Susannah counted in her head, "One little second, two little seconds …" and so on. The worst method was Jonny's: he decided to count his pulse, a deeply flawed idea, given the tension and its inevitable effect on his heart rate. "I decided to take my pulse because it's usually bang on 60. But, and this was stupid, because of the tension I knew that it would be way up. I tried to compensate by taking 80 as a minute for the first five minutes and then bring it down. It was total bollocks."

The game was under way and the pressure mounted. It was a complete test of concentration and the ability to focus solely on counting. John failed, his concentration wandered when an ant ran over his foot and he feared it might bite him. "It's really easy to count if you just twitch. One minute was the little toe on the left and when it reached the little toe on the right that was ten. And it was really accurate but I just couldn't be sure if it was 20 minutes or 30 minutes and I just lost it somewhere between 30 or 40 minutes when a fire ant walked over my sandal. I thought it was going to bite me. I knew I was accurate because after 14 minutes they changed the tape in the cameras and then did it again after what I thought was 56 minutes but was actually 46 minutes. I couldn't remember whether it was 30 or 40 I had done. So when 50 minutes had gone, I thought it was a full hour and the tape was changed at 56. Then when I got up I worked out that it was 46. I was only 30 seconds from 50 minutes. I had to stand there like an idiot knowing that I had blown it. Then when it went over a minute I was willing Jonny to move."

When John stood up, people were astonished: he was way early. The next crucial point would come around the hour mark – who would stand up first. It now became a test of nerve, or bottle. It would be easy to sit there and wait for the other to stand up, count a minute after that and hope that would get you nearer. Far braver to have the courage to trust your instincts and stand up when you believed an hour was up.

As members of the crew glanced furtively at their watches out of sight of the contestants, the hour passed. The person who stood up now would win. The atmosphere was as tense as it had ever been on either series of *Survivor*. As the minutes and seconds passed by, it became clear that John was back in with a chance: if neither Susannah and Jonny got up before nine minutes and 52 seconds had elapsed after the hour then John would win, almost by default. All of a sudden, Susannah got up and lit her torch. She had won. Jonny waited a minute but he was too late. Susannah had won immunity. John knew it as well and would tell her on the way back, though no one could be sure, especially when Mark told them he would not reveal the winner until Tribal Council the next evening.

"We came away with a feeling of anti-climax because we thought it would be really dramatic and climactic," she remembers. "It might have been for those watching it but for us it was a guess. We had really enjoyed the challenges and we had come out of them with a real sense of frustration and disappointment or a real sense of elation and pride. It wasn't a matter of that this time; it was a matter of concentration. We all wanted to win. I had total respect for John and Jonny. I did feel confident that both would take me through. While I counted I remember slowing down, which is why I went so far past an hour. The fire and sunshine were quite hypnotic. I thought John was around 16 minutes early.

"I stuck to my method, even though it wasn't best getting up in the middle, before Jonny. The boys told me they thought I had won but I wasn't sure. I wanted to believe them. But I started thinking then about what I would do if I did win. I said on camera that I didn't know who I was going to take through up until the last minute, even though I did know all the time I was going to take Jonny through because I made that promise with him. Both of us had decided, and it may have been Jonny not wanting to reveal on camera that he was scheming with me, that we would not talk about our promise on camera because if it got back to John then it would trouble him. He was a mate of ours as well and we did not want him to think we were going behind his back."

Hearing John state that he was confident gave Jonny the impression that his days on the island were numbered and he would be leaving the next evening. "When John jumped up I thought, 'That's way early.' Then I was thinking about what I should do next. I was thinking that, no matter what, I will come up last. My thinking was that John was way early, then Susannah would get up and she would be early and then if I gave it a minute I would be nearer by a minute. I carried on counting but John had floored me by getting up and I lost my way a bit. I thought when Susannah got up it was close to a minute and I just hoped she was a bit before and I was nearer. But when I thought back afterwards I knew she'd won. John thought the same. Then I thought I've just got to accept that I came third and that it was an enjoyable experience.

"I thought she would take John through because she said that if she reached the final two then she thought John would get the guys' votes, but that she would get Drew, Helen and Bridget's votes. However, she said that if she were up against me then I would get both the guys' and the girls' votes. She said she had more chance of winning against John so I just assumed she would get rid of me when she won that last immunity."

The atmosphere back at the camp was quiet. It was certain that the next 24 hours would pass very slowly. John and Jonny both reiterated to the camera that they would stick by each other. The bond was unshakeable: they were born on the same day, had bought the same first single ("D.I.S.C.O." by the tragic dance troop Ottowan) and had similarly atrocious tastes in music. They would be friends, so both insist, for life, whether one of them won the million pounds or not. They had many things in common and neither was willing to put that friendship at risk, even for a million pounds. They had become so close.

Susannah told the camera that she had not made up her mind, although she now claims she had. The million pounds was beginning to become increasingly important. She is not like some of the other contestants, who pretended they were there for the experience and not the million, an easy comment to make when you are sitting drinking beer on the jury and you have lost. No, she was there for the experience and the money. "I have found over the last few years that I have got a lot of student loans and graduate loans and a massive mortgage and credit-card bills. On a teacher's salary I cannot see that I am going to be able to clear all that and that has been weighing me down an awful lot. The million pounds would allow me to start afresh."

Interestingly, she said that it was difficult for her to decide which of the two she got on better with, but she now makes it clear that it was Jonny. "Jonny is a rock as far as I'm concerned," she said. "Throughout the whole experience he has been extremely funny and always looked on the bright side, always willing to chivvy you on, chip in to make sure everyone's spirits are high. He worked really hard throughout … he has been a really good friend. I think the flip side for him is that sometimes I see real anger in him and perhaps frustration … and perhaps I don't have as much in common with him as I do with John, like books we have read and things like that." The questions she was asked in that interview, about people's negative and positive qualities, upset Susannah. "I found it hard," she told Jonny and John. Jonny thought it amusing, prompting Susannah to poke fun at his bleached blonde hair. "Did you bleach it because you were going grey?" she teased. "No, it's because I thought blondes would have more fun … I was trying to look like Marilyn Monroe."

According to John, it was a "horrible night", partly because of the tension and partly because his illness was worsening by the second. The next day, day thirty-five, he was fit for little other than sleeping. "It was a horrible night. I couldn't sleep. I was thinking of the million pounds because I thought whomever she took through would win the million and I felt sure she would pick me because I was less popular. The next day I felt so rough I didn't do anything, while they took the boat out. I had been with Susannah for five weeks and there was nothing I could do to influence her decision. I was friendly towards her but I didn't click in the same way she and Jonny did – there was a bit of chemistry there to be sure. There was nothing at all between me and Susannah."

John's confidence was in evidence at that nail-biting Tribal Council. Asked by Mark about their alliance, he mentioned Bridget and how much she had helped them throughout the course of the game, a gratuitous piece of flattery and a blatant attempt to try to win her vote on the jury. For a second, when the results of the Immunity Challenge were read out, John suddenly thought he had won because of the way they were revealed.

His first instinct was right, however, and Susannah won her first immunity victory, and stepped forward to accept the amulet. She told Mark it was "a mixed blessing." As John could only vote for Jonny and vice versa their votes cancelled each other out so the only person whose vote counted was Susannah. As she walked to the end of the platform to vote, she paused before writing. "I can honestly say," she intoned gravely, "that this is the most difficult thing that I have had to do during my entire *Survivor* experience." It made gutting a cayman seem pleasurable in comparison.

For those watching on the screens in the gallery, the tension was almost unbearable. People were convinced that she would vote for Jonny to go, giving her the best chance of winning the million. Against Jonny, people fathomed, she did not stand a chance. As she wrote, a "J" and an "O" people were fully expecting to see her scribble an "N". But instead there was an "H" and then an "N". Everyone was still reeling when she held the paper to the camera and said she was voting John off and taking through "her bestest buddy" to the final.

Friendship had won over avarice. Susannah, whom

everyone had thought would be ruthless, whom everyone had labelled ambitious, who had a book in which her husband urged her to shaft everyone, had stepped back from another betrayal. "Up until that point all the voting had been collective, but all of a sudden the responsibility was on me alone," she says now. "That was not nice. I thought about whether I was making the right decision, because I thought both the boys might have a better chance than I had, because Al and Dave wanted a guy to win and also they both got on with them. I felt that John and Jonny would get the boys' votes and I'm not sure about Drew and Helen. Possibly, I thought, it would not make a difference who I took through to the final and I wanted to keep to my word. It was horrible to see John go and I was really upset because I was responsible for saying, in essence, 'F*ck off'."

As Susannah made her way back, John and Jonny waited, having already wished each other luck. As Mark pulled the vote from the urn, Jonny put his hand behind his back and on his rucksack, ready to haul it on to his shoulders and leave. He had no speech or last goodbyes prepared, he was just going to go. On the other side of Susannah, John wiped the sweat from his palms on his trousers, in preparation for offering a consolatory handshake to his friend. When Mark revealed his name, both were stunned. The unbreakable bond had been shattered. John hugged Susannah, punched Jonny on the fists and said, "Walk on Bruce".

"I was ready to leave," Jonny recalls. "I remember thinking that I was going to smile at them both, no hard-feelings sort of thing. I was convinced, utterly convinced. But then it came out as John and I was amazed. I was flabbergasted. Then I thought, 'Oh no', I've been saying that she was really untrustworthy, yet she had stuck to what she said she would do, so I was really surprised. But I was also really happy, I think grateful is the word I would use. I was so grateful to her."

As they stood at the end of the jetty waiting to board their boat, Susannah, who had been in tears, turned to Jonny and said, "It was so hard seeing John go like that." Jonny said, "I'll speak to you when we get back to camp." He was delighted and spent the whole boat journey thanking Susannah profusely for what she had just done. He told her that he thought she would take John through. When she asked "Why?" "I just thought you would," was Jonny's response. "But I said to you that I'd take you through," Susannah insisted. Jonny was embarrassed to say, but he told her why he had doubted her. "I thought you were more ambitious than you were; it wasn't anything you said, any lies you had told or anything. There was just something about you I didn't trust."

Susannah was horrified. "I said to him, 'Don't be bloody stupid. I've told you ever since day seven that I would take you through and of course I would do it.' On the way back he was massively elated. It dawned on us that we were the final two. It was extraordinary. He kept thanking me. It was weird but we stayed up talking until 2am because we were both on such a high. Jonny was running through what he would wear for the last show, whether he should he wear his kilt. Even though John had gone we were on a high. We talked through the whole thing about John."

John was in a state of shock, and was also extremely unwell, but he managed to give an articulate and witty interview to Mark. He paid tribute to Jonny. "He is incredibly gregarious and charismatic and he gelled with everyone and he had a little moment of his day set aside for everyone, so he was quite shrewd in that respect, so I think he has a very good chance." The only thing that puzzled him was Stephen Flett's assertion that he had practised for the log stand at home by standing on his sofa for hours on end. "I don't know where he got that from," John says now, "it makes me sound really sad. I swear I never said it – he must have dreamt it or something."

John accepts that his blind loyalty to his tribe and the alliances he made cost him a million pounds. At that stage, he was interested only in getting off to a bed and some paracetamol. After arriving back in England he had a chance to look back and analyse how it went. He has one regret about the way he played the game, and that was not allowing Bridget to win the Orientation Island Challenge. "I'm happy with the third place but I hadn't really thought what I would do at the end because I didn't expect to get that far. I wasn't shrewd enough at the end, I think. You need a strategy like Susannah had, because it's difficult to do it when you are there and know the people. I wish I had thought it all the way through before I went. I never actually said to Susannah that I wouldn't vote against her, like I did with Jonny. So maybe I should've got rid of her. My main regret was not to make sure that Bridget won the island game. I considered it but I'm a natural show-off and had to win. I couldn't resist it." He does believe that Jonny and Susannah were worthy finalists. "He's a tough competitor and a great guy and she's a strong woman. She had done a lot of preparation in every way, more than anyone, so she deserved it."

John can console himself with the fact that he was by far the best competitor in the challenges. At times he was unstoppable and, if every challenge had been a test of athleticism, he would have won them all. His accomplishments had more than made up for his overweening arrogance on some challenges, though his compulsive need to show off will not endear him to many. But as a wit and raconteur he provided a great deal of entertainment as well, and his one-liners and self-deprecating wit often had everyone contestants and crew alike – in hysterics. Even after he had been voted off, and was still suffering from his sickness, he was still cracking jokes. During a run through for the final Tribal Council, when the jury were filmed walking down the platform to vote for the benefit of the cameras, John approached the voting station. He picked up the pen and wrote "Ed" on a piece of paper, then held up and intoned the series editor's name solemnly into the camera. The laugh from the gallery could be heard back in Bocas. He provided shafts of humour even when the weather was at its worst and conditions were grim.

Back at the camp he was missed. Susannah told the camera that her decision was swayed by having spent the day with Jonny when John was confined to his sick bed. Though she realised her chances of winning were slim, she was still delighted. "At this moment I feel overwhelmed that I am in the final two of *Survivor*. I cannot believe it. I was coming back in the boat with Jonny and both of us had our heads up to the sky, looking at the stars, going 'Oh my God'. It is becoming more surreal as time progresses. It is tremendously exciting and if I don't win the million I will have got such a sense of achievement for getting this far and I know if Jonny wins it then it couldn't go to a nicer guy."

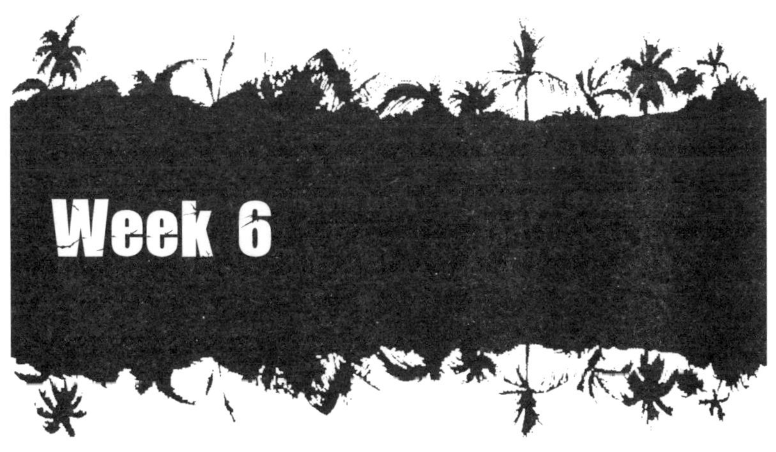

Posh and Cheques

When Susannah and Jonny woke the next day, the events of the night before were still on their minds. They had only managed two hours' sleep, thoughts whirling around their minds about the final and what the future entailed. Day thirty-six stretched out ahead of them, with very little for them to do other than think about the speeches they would make and try to avoid spending the million pounds in their heads. There were no challenges, a few interviews to do to camera, but apart from that their time was their own. Being the last two was strange – the shelter felt huge, the island massive. Both felt immense pride when they looked around and saw they were the two who had gone the whole distance and would see every sunset and sunrise.

Despite this realisation the day was long and, in many respects, boring. Given that there were only two days to go there seemed little point in fishing, though they made a cursory effort. It was also too early to start preparing their speeches. Susannah had the advantage in that respect, having won pen and paper on which to write her speech in the "Fallen

Comrades" challenge. But she decided to wait until the following afternoon before even thinking of what she might say. Before John had been voted off, the three of them had agreed that the speeches might not make a great deal of difference, people's minds already being made up in advance. What would be more important, they deduced, would be the answers they supplied to the questions of the jury.

As they idled away the hours, the jury were being split up. They had congregated at 'The Buccaneer' before being moved to a beach house on El Limbo, a short walk down the beach from Tribal Council. Here they could sunbathe, drink beer and eat to their hearts' content. But Ed Forsdick wanted people to think deeply about the very important decision they would have to make and he reasoned they would do that better in isolation. So on day thirty-six they were taken to Bocas and put in separate hotels, including John who was still feeling weak, and told to cogitate over their questions and their decisions. Knowing the jury members were in and around Bocas, the crew were told that certain bars they frequented were off-limits to avoid both parties meeting and discussing the vote over a frozen margarita.

Each jury member was interviewed about their thoughts on the upcoming Tribal Council and their opinions of each finalist. Drew spoke very warmly about Jonny and how she had got to know him on the deep sea fishing reward. "He seems genuine," she added. "I relate to him because he is a police officer." She could not come up with a single flaw. She was more suspicious of Susannah. "She is a nice person, very intelligent and very clever, but I wonder sometimes whether we all got to see the real Susannah. For instance, at Tribal Council when Mark asked her questions, her answers seemed almost rehearsed. Of course, they weren't. I just wonder sometimes about her." For Drew, what was vital was that the winner should be someone with honesty and integrity. Jonny's "magic" on the boat while fishing appeared to have worked.

Bridget was more focused on who would benefit most from winning the money, and who would be most likely to give it to charity. This seemed to be good news for Susannah, who supports the same breast cancer charity, ABC, as Bridget. In fact, they had a common acquaintance. "Susannah's uncle is one of the leading figures in the charity and the lady I deal with knows her family very well, so within a week of being on the island we had established that we had a common link." Unlike the others, she was able to look past Susannah's accent and articulacy. "I don't think she's posh, I think she is great," she said emphatically. But her heart was torn because she also felt fondly about Jonny, especially the way he had coped with the death of his mother when he was younger. "He is very funny. I would like to go out one night with him and have a 'sesh', although I think I would be floored first. He is one of the most genuine people I have met in a very long time. I know some of the others thought there was another side to Susannah but obviously I know differently. She is a very genuine person."

Sincerity and a strong moral code were the main attributes Helen was looking for, together with someone who had shared a similar upbringing to her, which would be nigh on impossible given that she lives within spitting distance of 57 cousins. In particular, she wanted someone who had been honest the whole way through. Jonny had made a big impression on her during the Ambassador's Visit, making her feel at ease and giving her all the information she needed. Ironically, this was where Susannah might have made a negative impression on the other tribe, despite the fact that she was acting on orders cooked up by Jonny and John. Like Drew, her friend, she was unable to cite any flaws in Jonny's character. Susannah, however, she liked but she did not believe had been as honest and forthcoming as the others. "When we do have a conversation," she added, "she is witty and bright and I feel intimidated by that. When I sit and talk to Susannah, I feel that she has given a lot of thought to what she will say before she replies and I find that quite unusual."

Alastair, ever the diplomat – during *Survivor* he spent as much time on the fence as he did on the log – prized sincerity above all else, and he felt Jonny was sincere. But he did have reservations about his fellow Scotsman. "Jonny is a very likeable chap, but he can be a bit aloof. He can be too diplomatic for my liking, though he's an extremely nice guy and the kind of guy I get on with tremendously." Susannah, on one hand, was a "lovely girl". But on the other hand he felt she was "lacking sincerity". "She is a very intelligent girl and I think she has thought ahead of the game a lot more than Jonny but I still find her quite aloof and insincere in comparison."

Dave was the only one who appeared to be keeping an open mind until he had heard what people would say at Tribal Council, though that could simply have been for the benefit of the camera. He was going to wait to hear their speeches and the answers to the questions he had devised. "Jonny's a smashing feller. He's a down-to-earth man and he's also very witty and funny at times. The downside to him is that he can make someone laugh one minute but then an hour later he can call them worse than something, so really there could be a two-faced side to Jonny that I haven't really seen a lot." Predictably, the word "posh" cropped up frequently when Dave was quizzed about Susannah. "She even swears posh," he said incredulously. "Susannah, she's very bubbly and straightforward and she seems to like everybody and that I'm scared of because I don't believe that anybody is that perfect."

Dragged from his sick bed, John, as probably the person who knew the finalists best, was able to offer his insights, free from any bitterness. He appeared to have got over his disappointment well. "Jonny is incredibly caring. He'd wake up in the shelter every morning and the first thing he would ask everybody, regardless of where they had come from, was whether they were all right. He is also incredibly childish, which appealed to my childish nature. On the log challenge we spent 24 hours talking gibberish." Against him was the fact he could be disingenuous, for example the way he made Bridget believe she would be his friend for life when he had said a number of poisonous remarks behind her back. "He exaggerated his friendliness," John added.

For Susannah, the woman who voted him off, he had nothing but the greatest respect. "She's incredibly self-assured for 27; mature beyond her years. Jonny would get nervous before the games but Susannah would blossom before them and become very self-confident. The downside of that was that when she won the immunities she became insufferably confident, almost to the point of being slightly arrogant." It's a surprise John did not choke on these words, given they were criticisms often levelled at himself. He did make a prescient point, however, about Susannah sometimes losing her audience around the camp. "She wouldn't moderate her conversation, and that can be an admirable quality, but when she was talking to Dave about a full-bodied red or Chopin's piano concerto, I could see she was losing him because he wasn't of that ilk." Now, if she had pontificated on the merits of Brown Ale and the works of Lindisfarne then she would have got Dave's vote in the bag.

Day thirty-six seemed interminable for Susannah and Jonny and it was a blessed relief when they went to bed. When the next day dawned, they attempted to fish but the visibility was poor and the will, as Susannah admits, had gone. Home was foremost in their minds. "It was funny – the desire to survive had gone because the end was nigh," she says. "We just wanted it over and done with and to eat some nice food and drink beer and then get home because we were both missing our partners. I had the pen and paper and it was a miserable day, really wet and cold. Eventually, I ended up writing mine at one end of the shelter, Jonny at the other. As I wrote it, my overriding aim was to get over that I had put every single bit of effort into this game and that I had not ridden on anyone's coat-tails; that I had tried my hardest and brought all my skills to this and that I would do constructive things with the cash. I knew they thought I was posh and privileged and I wanted to put across that I was me and had been all the way through."

Jonny was dreading the evening, public speaking not being a skill of his. He also knew that he would find it difficult to match Susannah. "I knew Susannah would be a better speaker than I was; she's used to it in school. I knew her speech would include the effort she made before coming to the island and what she had put into it. I thought that I wouldn't try to match that, or say you should vote for me instead of her because of this. I spoke to John before the final three and we talked about the speeches and we thought the same: that we wouldn't do anybody else down in any way. I decided to go along the lines that they had all made their minds up, they knew me and what my humour is and there was nothing I could do or say to change their minds."

The speeches completed, they tidied the beach. They took down the Columbus flag and halved it. They also decided to burn down the shelter, not out of any latent pyromania but because they wanted to return the island to its natural state. Despite the growing tension ahead of the Tribal Council, the pair were still joking with each other. "If you win the million," said Jonny, "then I'm going to find out where you live and come and slash your tyres on all six of your new cars." "And burn down all three of my houses," replied Susannah. "Then I'll tell Barney that I had a mad passionate affair with you but you also had Dave, Alastair, John … and Drew and Sarah."

The stage was set for Tribal Council. On the face of it, Jonny appeared to be the most popular so it would require a speech of Churchillian proportions from Susannah to disabuse most of the jury members of the view that she was insincere and too posh. Jonny, meanwhile, wanted to keep his speech understated; all he could do was blow it with a wrong answer. He had played the "Grey Man" to perfection. On both series, many contestants have made clear their wish to be the person who slips under the radar, who doesn't make themselves conspicuous. Jonny is the only one who has been able to pursue that strategy successfully, befriending everyone without alienating others, performing strongly in the challenges without being too much of a threat, and staying true to his alliances without being diverted, however tempted he might have been. His opening speech was an excellent summary of his appeal. He singled out members of the jury and gave his lasting impression of them, flattering them all in various ways. It was a cunning strategy. In fact, his only error occurred in his opening statement. Comparing the importance of the decision of a *Survivor* jury debating whether to award someone a million pounds to that of a jury deciding on someone's freedom stretches credulity.

"Guys, I've stood in front of juries in many serious cases in the past. However, I firmly believe you have as much responsibility as any juror that I've ever been in front of because at the end of the day, your decision will change one of our lives for the rest of our lives. I'm not going to try to sway your vote because I believe over the last 37 days you've already probably already firmly made up your minds and I feel you've all lived with me for a while. You've known me for 37 days, most of you, and you know what my humour is and you know what I'm like and you know what I think and you know what I'm about. Instead, I'm going to concentrate on each of you and tell each of you what my lasting memory will be.

"Starting with Helen: I've been in the police for ten years and I've never met anyone with half the frequency or severity of swearing. I've never heard it from anyone in my life before, let alone a 22-year-old blonde girl. You say your Mum's worse. I find that almost impossible to believe.

"Alastair: Firstly, it's got to be your size 27 feet, especially on that log. Your heels and toes were off at the same time. You're a giant of a man and when we were in the shelter and you needed a bathroom stop in the middle of the night, the whole shelter shook as soon as you stood up.

"Drew: You've got faster hands than Fagin. When you won the Reward Challenge after I gave you a black eye and some of the times on that boat will be some of the funniest memories I've got of the whole *Survivor* experience.

"Dave: There are two things in particular I will remember about you: your immense willpower during the "Hands-up" barrel challenge – I thought that was incredible. Secondly, when you were shouting to your son Robert in the boat, you asked him three questions: first, what was the score on Saturday; second, where are Newcastle in the league; and then last of all you remembered to ask how your wife was. You're a true man's man, there's no doubt about that.

"Bridget: It would have to be your immense energy that you had every morning. I think I know more about your family and your entire family history than I do my own. And I think I know more about your sex life than I do about my own as well.

"And finally John: We've had more top five lists for more subjects that I even knew existed. Also your immense one-liners. I'm not going to say much more as your head will end up the same size as mine. One thing I do want to forget, if possible, was the YMCA rendition that we did on South Island but I think that's one thing that you or I will never, ever be allowed to forget. I'm going to shut up now as I'm sure you've got some questions for the both of us."

Brief and to the point, yet with a word for everybody, and all said with a broad smile on his face, it was classic Jonny. We can only imagine what the response would have been had he said what he truly thought. "Alastair, you're devious and I don't trust you one inch," or "Bridget, you did my head in," might not have won him many votes. It was a tough act for Susannah to follow, which she acknowledged.

"I would just like to say how gorgeous you all look this evening and I hope I can get half way there after tonight's bed and breakfast, which I'm very much looking forward to. The first thing that I would say, is that I feel immensely privileged to be standing here tonight as part of the final two on *Survivor*. I'm also really privileged to be standing in front of six people who have made the last few weeks of my life the most unforgettable. I think I can really clearly say that and I think that most of you will agree. When I applied to come on *Survivor* the two things that I said were most important to me were the experience of the whole thing and the challenge, mentally and physically. I put money fairly down the list because it seemed to me a distant dream and I never dared hope I would be in the final two and in with a chance of winning. My two aims were, firstly, not to be the first person voted off because I didn't want to suffer the humiliation, but also having given up my job I wanted to make the most of having six full weeks in the experience and on the programme itself. I also wanted to be on the jury because I wanted the chance of influencing who might win this vast amount. I hoped it might be someone genuine who had given 100 per cent to the experience and also would do something positive with the money and not just for themselves.

"From the start I really believe that I threw myself into the experience, doing lots of research at home, even breaking various bits of the skirting board and trying to make fire, which my husband didn't really approve of. As soon as I joined my tribe I was lucky enough to be with a group of people who worked hard, if not harder than me sometimes, foraging for food, lugging logs around and rowing as much as I could. The challenges have been incredible and I think everyone will agree. I'm just so chuffed to be part of a group of people that have given their all to them. I know that sometimes you have seen me as an arty-farty teacher with a posh accent and I hope that I've come across as myself, as never pretending to be anything that I wasn't and always giving everything I have to the whole experience.

"To be honest, today I spent about an hour in the shelter writing down hundreds and hundreds of words on a piece of paper – I was just enjoying the feeling of having a pen and paper in my hand – and after about an hour I put them down and I said to Jonny, 'This is the biggest load of rubbish that I have ever written in my life. These people have been with me the whole time. They know who I am. Nothing I can say can sway them either way. Ultimately, they are going to vote with their heads and with their hearts.' I totally respect whatever decision you make. Jonny, in true fashion, said, 'Well, Suze, it probably doesn't matter either way. You'd probably be better off showing them your boobs and then sitting down again.' Well, I haven't quite done that – I haven't got any boobs left to show, but I wouldn't anyway. Thankfully, I am going to sit down now and just hope that our beer and sandwiches come very quickly. Thank you for your time."

Then it was the time for questions; perhaps the most important part of the evening. The contestants approached the stand in the order they were voted off, so Helen went first, with two questions for each finalist. She addressed Susannah first, asking which members of Columbus she got along with least. Susannah is full of praise for this question; it certainly put her on the spot. In effect, she was going to have to single out two members of the jury. She, smartly, selected the two who were unlikely to vote for her anyway; the two she believed would not vote for any woman – Dave and Alastair.

"I would like to pick out one person who is most different from me and I think, Dave, you and I have sometimes been like chalk and cheese. You from the north of England, liking your footie and the rest of it, and me from the south only ever having been dragged to a football match kicking and screaming by my Dad once. I'd like to think that, even if we do have our differences, we do appreciate the same things in life, beauty of sunsets, things like that. I really admire your strengths, all the way, especially in the holding onto the barrel challenge ('Hands-up') and even though we are different I would never say that I disliked you, quite the contrary. I really admire your strengths and determination. I think it's very hard to pick people because we know that we've all said that we've got on very well and I think that's true."

She then paused as she tried to find the easiest route out of further weakening her already slim chances. "The second person is very difficult to choose and I might have to say Alastair purely because of our difference in backgrounds. I don't have any of your military experience to share and I haven't been able to share in your stories but I've enjoyed them when you told them." Helen thanked her for that answer and then gave her the opportunity to nail the view that she was an upper-middle-class rich kid who had never gone wanting in her life by asking her why she, Helen, should vote for a person with a much more privileged upbringing.

"I think first of all appearances can be deceiving," answered Susannah. "I don't think anyone should take anything on face value. I know and I knew before I came along that my accent might give people the impression that I'm pretentious or a snob or am better off than I actually am. I hope that I've been as genuine as I could be and that I've shown you all that I'm an honest, open person and I would never lie to anybody about my background or financial situation." She did not say it, but it seemed clear she was referring to Alastair.

"Unfortunately," she continued, "I am not as financially secure as my accent may give me away to be. Yes, I've had a fortunate upbringing but no more so than a lot of people sitting on the jury. My student loans and debts and my graduate loans and my credit-card bills that I've got, I don't see how I could ever pay off with my teacher's salary at the moment." It was a bold attempt but it was unlikely to sway many people's opinions.

Then it was Jonny's turn to be under fire. Pointedly, Helen remembered how the agreement made by Alastair, John and Jonny on the log led directly to her eviction. "Why should I help you?" she added. "The agreement on the log was between myself, Alastair and John and was made about the twenty-first hour. I'm sure that you would agree with me that it seemed unfair that, later on that evening, John or Alastair was going to be voted off when they had put in so much effort. It was obvious to both tribes, I think, that John would be the natural target for North Island and Alastair would be the natural for South Island. We were open about that, we discussed it, and we all three agreed that it would be unfair that anyone who had put in so much effort on the log should be up for eviction. The same with Susannah; she had stood there for 17 hours and similarly I felt that the effort she had put in was incredible and that purely left Bridget from our team. We felt that, as Bridget was the maternal figure from South Island and you were the maternal figure from North Island, it would be best to put the two of you head-to-head and I hope that explains it."

Jonny cleverly avoided the real reason – that they were the weakest – but that might not have played well with Helen. If she was looking for honesty and sincerity, she had not yet found it from Jonny. "So why should I vote for you now?" she asked next. "I hope you vote for me now because I've been playing the game; there was nothing malicious in it, there was nothing personal. I was purely trying to play the game the best I could and I knew that if Bridget was up against somebody then I thought the best person would be the other person who is seen as the maternal figure." Of course, it was personal on his and John's behalf, but their ire was directed at Bridget. Had he confessed to that, Bridget would have been shocked, and had he described Helen as weak her vote might have gone the other way. Cleverly, he had put a positive spin on his answer.

Then it was Alastair's turn. He was puzzled by Susannah's reluctance to side with Dave when he approached her about forming an alliance. "When John said it was an unbreakable alliance three days ago (at Tribal Council) I firmly believe that he meant that John and Jonny and I had formed an alliance in the early days that we had promised each other that we would carry through until the final three. Unfortunately, I had to vote somebody off because I was given the fortunate or unfortunate position of being the person that had to stop someone from the chance of winning a million pounds. And I firmly believe that those people that I had made a promise to and who had become very, very firm friends were people that I should stick with to the end, even though it may perhaps hinder my chances of winning the million pounds. I felt that my word to both of them was the most important thing. And even though Dave approached me, and rightly so because everybody should have the chance of getting as far as I have done, I felt that my bond with John and Jonny should be cemented and kept to."

"But the way I see it," Alastair responded, "it was a bond between John and Jonny. Do you feel you had equal status in that bond?" Alastair's interpretation was correct but, the way Susannah saw it, he was wrong and she said so. Alastair then asked why she decided on Jonny rather than John as her partner in the final two. "I can honestly say that was the most difficult point of my time on *Survivor*, having to take the responsibility and personally being responsible for stopping one of them having the chance of winning a million pounds. It was extremely unpleasant. Up to that point, I think all of us had thought about voting collectively and nobody had to take that responsibility and I had to take one of the two. Between the two, it was very difficult because they are both excellent competitors and to be quite honest I did not do it on tactics. I did it perhaps because I feel I have a stronger friendship with Jonny than with John but it's very, very difficult because I felt that my friendship with both of them was strong. It was perhaps at the end of it a slight gut reaction, but an extremely difficult decision."

Alastair's next two questions were about whether Susannah had said anything uncomplimentary about anyone on camera, which she managed to parry. He followed up by inquiring about the extravagances she would treat herself to if she won a million. Reasoning that it may not be politic to mention her bath of champagne at this forum, she said extravagances came well down her list of priorities – which might have been difficult for some to swallow, knowing how enamoured Susannah was of the finer things in life. "I would love to buy myself a spanking new bike because that is my main method of transport and at the moment it is a rusty old model that I know will never get nicked. In fact, two bikes: a nice racer and a really, really fantastic mountain bike with suspension and gears and the works." Then with a grin she added, "Perhaps a small house on one of the Italian lakes as well."

To Jonny, Alastair put the question that John had said their alliance was between the two of them and was unbreakable, while Susannah had said it was a threesome, so what was the right answer? Jonny replied that his initial alliance was with John and then Susannah. Alastair then asked the big question: who would he have taken through to the final, Susannah or John? "If I had won immunity two days ago I would have taken John through to the final because I had given him my word first."

Susannah could not believe it. She felt, she says, "completely betrayed". As Jonny sat down after telling Alastair that he would buy a Bang and Olufsen stereo and an Edinburgh townhouse with his winnings – although bizarrely he wasn't asked if he had been uncomplimentary about anybody on camera, as Susannah was – Susannah shot him a filthy look. She made a note to confront him about his duplicity afterwards.

"He was thinking of John's vote," she says now, "but he has subsequently said to me that he was convinced that I would not take him through, that I wasn't being completely honest. Therefore, he was unsure of what I would do but when I did take him through he was eternally grateful and realised that he was wrong. He told me that usually he trusts his gut reaction but that he did get me wrong, even though I had promised him all the way through."

While Susannah tried to contain her anger with Jonny, Drew was at the stand and speaking about how she admired honesty. Her question asked what they thought their three best qualities were, starting with Susannah, to whom she said, perhaps mindful that the bars in Bocas would be closing soon, "if you can try and be direct and not waffle". Susannah listed her qualities as being trusting, determined and inventive. Jonny listed honesty, citing his refusal to lie about his job; friendliness, and last of all how caring he was and laid it on by going on to say how he had too much feeling for everyone, especially children, "if I see them being brought up wrongly". Happy, Drew left the stand to be replaced by Dave, who had taken this part of the game seriously.

His first question was to Jonny, asking if he would leave the police force. "My immediate reaction is yes, without a shadow of a doubt," Jonny replied, though after the show it might not have been in question whether he would leave or be asked to leave. "I would have to think more carefully about that. I would certainly take some time to let it settle and get through my head. I would certainly take a year out, anyway, and think seriously. It has been part of my life for ten years. There have always been loads of parts I have enjoyed, really enjoyed, but I have always wished I had done more travelling. I haven't been to a lot of places really. I wish I had gone travelling at 18 or 19 as most people have done." He went on to say he had thought about becoming a physiotherapist because of his interest in fitness, and that he would consider going to university.

Dave then asked him about serving the public and could he just walk away like that? "I think working with the police after winning a million in such a public manner would be very difficult," he said sagely. "I think one of my best attributes in the police is that I get on well with criminals, all people from different walks of life, and I think people would find it difficult to be open knowing that you have a million quid sitting in your bank account."

Susannah was asked if she had ever suffered any deprivation. "I think everybody has experienced deprivation in life. I think it would be wrong for anybody to assume that nobody had suffered sorrow or loss or difficulties in life. I certainly have. I would be lying if I said that I didn't have a reasonably comfortable upbringing. I have two parents who are very happily still in love after 30 years of marriage and I was brought up with my brother in just an average middle-class situation. It was a really good start to my life and I think a lot of my strengths have come from the fact that I had a really positive start in life. At times when I have lost close friends due to deaths, even sudden deaths, when they were young, and also have experienced problems and sorrows with my immediate family, and my husband's family, those times have been very difficult to get through. I haven't necessarily shared them with people on the jury, and with the camera and national television, because they are intensely personal, but I tried to get through those as best I can. I think one of the reasons I have chosen the vocation of teaching in a state school is because I want to give back some of the things I had as a child to other people who haven't had such an easy upbringing and working with a lot of children in very difficult situations has made me understand how immensely lucky I have been earlier in my life and how much I have to give to those people who haven't had such a great start in life."

Nearly all the questions addressed to Susannah so far seemed to have been about class. It had become almost an obsession among members of the jury, the belief that she was stinking rich and had only gone on *Survivor* to become richer. There seemed little she could do to dispel that, other than admit she had a good upbringing and hope that wasn't seen as a crime. But her voice and vocabulary put up an almost insurmountable barrier: she spoke well therefore she must be loaded, seemed to be the common view. People spoke of her having a "sting in the tail", yet when the end came she had surprised everyone and stuck to her word, even at the expense of winning. She did not help herself in the way that she treated Lee and, as John says, she could have moderated the way she communicated with some members of Columbus, but in many respects she has every reason to feel hard done by. Most of the questions she received at the final Tribal Council were far more hostile than the ones patted over the net for Jonny to smash home. But then Jonny made friends more easily and *Survivor* is nothing if not a popularity contest.

Dave questioned Jonny about what three changes, starting with the least momentous, would befall him should he take the top prize. Jonny named his personality as the thing about him that would alter least, saying he would still frequent the same bars and pubs, regardless. He mentioned giving some money to his nephew and his sister and the rest of his family. "The most important change," he continued, "is that I am now 31 and I should try to think of settling down sooner or later. I have always wanted to live in Edinburgh, and didn't want to move out of Edinburgh, and if I was in the police and I had kids I would have to move out to the suburbs. I didn't want to do that if I could possibly afford it and this would let me think about having a family sooner than planned and still be able to live in Edinburgh and give them a comfortable lifestyle as well. So thinking about having a family would be the most important thing."

For Susannah, the least important change involved settling her debts. "Similarly to Jonny," she added, "I don't want to start a family with the amount of debts I have at the moment." Secondly, she would sort out any financial troubles her family faced and start a trust fund for Barney's little brother and sister. "The third thing I would do, and this is really important to me, is help the charity that I have been working with for the last ten years, which is 'Action against Breast Cancer' (ABC). If I won this amount of money I would spend a lot of it on myself but I would feel it had been entirely wasted if I hadn't done something really concrete to help other people with it. That is a charity I have worked with for a very long time so I know the money would go to a very good cause."

After Dave was Bridget, who asked Jonny if he would have played the game differently had the prize been a few thousand pounds and not a million. "I wouldn't be as nervous as I am now if it had been for just a few thousand," Jonny joked. "But no, even if there had been no money involved in this game whatsoever I would still have played the same. I have found the whole thing an amazing experience and I would have applied for it from the start, even had there been no reward."

Susannah was asked if she had any regrets about the game and whether, hand on heart, she had been honest and truthful with fellow members of Columbus tribe. Her two regrets were her mistake in the first Immunity Challenge that cost South Island victory and allowing the chicken to escape after merger on day sixteen. "I think you were brilliant then," she told Bridget. "You came up to me and said, 'Don't worry about it,' and I had the camera pushed in my face and I was quite emotional, which was out of anger and frustration at my own stupidity." As for being truthful, she reckoned she had. "One of the things that has impressed me about *Survivor* is that I generally feel that people have been very honest. Now I may be wrong and it may be that I will be disproved when I watch the TV series, but I certainly believe that everyone has been more honest than I thought they would be."

Last to the stand before the closing speeches was John, who being a barrister was used to this sort of atmosphere. He even adopted a classic barrister's pose at the stand and the requisite furrowed brow. All that was required for him to complete the scene was to address Mark as "M'Lud". "I have actually been to more light-hearted murder trials than this has been tonight," he told Jonny and Susannah. "I bet you feel like Fred and Rosemary sitting there." His first question was to Jonny: given Jonny's "vulnerability" how would he cope with people attempting to take advantage of his new-found wealth?

"Just from being in the police for the past ten years I am well aware that most people aren't as nice and honest as they make out. I think I am quite a good judge of character and that is why I have bonded with a number of you. I do feel you are certainly a lot more honest and friendly than, for example, the people in the first *Survivor* series. I was expecting a number of people to be like that and I was really on the look out for that, but as far as I'm aware there has been no one like the people on *Survivor 1*. I know who my friends are and they have all been my friends for years and years and years and if anyone new came on the scene I would certainly be very wary of them. I think I am streetwise enough to be on the look-out for that." John then asked something that had been bugging him since he saw it. Why was Jonny taking his pulse during the "Time's Up" challenge? Jonny explained his thinking, to which John replied, "That's about as scientific as my approach."

He then turned to Susannah and asked her if she had considered the negative effects of winning a million and was she prepared for them? "I think even though I describe myself as arty-farty and may seem to be occasionally a bit pretentious, which I don't feel I am personally, I have got both feet firmly rooted on the ground. I have never had a million pounds so obviously I don't know the effects it will have on me. But one of the main reasons I came on *Survivor* was, as you yourself said, that I take nothing for granted and you realise how little you can live on personally, and how little people do live on in the world. Therefore, I think I would never take that amount of money for granted and I would always try and spend it wisely. I don't think it would have an adverse effect on my personality because my personality has been set for a long time now. I think one positive way that it would affect me is to make me feel happy and secure that I have done everything I can do for the people who I love and respect and who have supported me."

Had John been wearing glasses, he would have been looking over them at Susannah at this point. Like a mini Kavanagh QC, he leant over the stand and prayed forgiveness for his indulgence. "Susannah, you said you are not the sort of person who swaps and changes, but did you ever feel that your personality changed at all? After winning the Reward Challenge for example?" John had, on occasions, been perturbed by Susannah's smug manner after she had won a challenge or had done well. She managed to fend off John's "forensic" attack, though she resisted the temptation to say, "At least I didn't preen on the bar like a cocksure cockatoo in 'Hanging Around'."

"When I said my personality doesn't switch or change," she replied, "I mean the core values of my personality. Obviously, in this kind of experience you are going to experience highs and lows and I am sure everybody here can say they experienced them. I think my lowest point was the point when I felt physically unwell and I wasn't really winning anything, particularly in an alliance with you and Jonny who were very physically and mentally strong. I felt that I had to live up to the kind of record you set and that perhaps made me feel lower. The point where I actually did win a Reward Challenge did buoy me up and made me feel more confident and getting physically better helped as well. Perhaps with a smaller group of people, I felt happier and more at ease, but I would say the core values didn't change and that, essentially, I am me and always have been."

Questions over, it was time for the closing speeches. Susannah, to the relief of the jury, said she was going to keep her climax short. "I would just like to thank you for your questions because I think it gave me an opportunity to say a lot of things that I haven't been able to say and explain to you previously. Overall, I think that whatever happens tonight, hopefully you have got in front of you two people that you would be happy to see this amount of money going to, given that it is not yourselves. If you choose Jonny tonight you have a very worthy competitor and I wouldn't hold any grudge against you for choosing him. I would of course be honoured and delighted if you chose me, but I would like to say this has been an incredible time and I think all of us will hold those memories for the rest of our lives."

Jonny was even more succinct. "As I have said before on a few occasions, the whole experience for me has been amazing. I would like to thank the six of you for contributing towards that massively. I know you've got a massive decision to make tonight and I wish you luck in making the right one. Thanks for your time."

Before the jury could vote, the set was cleared of everyone apart from Technical Director Peter Johnston and Series Editor Ed Forsdick. Peter filmed each contestant's vote from a camera at the furthest end of the voting platform, with Ed behind him watching. The contestants voted one by one and John completed the process. Then the set was re-opened and the crew emerged from the jungle to film Mark telling the jury that the urn would be sealed and returned to the UK where it would be opened at the final live show. He then turned and walked away down the "path of fire". As the word "Cut" echoed around the set, Susannah turned to Jonny, eyes ablaze, and hissed, "You've got some explaining to do, mister!"

They were escorted down the beach to the house on El Limbo, while the jury were ferried back to their hotels in Bocas. Susannah was fuming at what she believed was Jonny's betrayal of their promise. Jonny tried to explain but she replied, "'No, I don't even want to hear about it now. You can wait." She says she wanted to make him suffer. Once inside the house, she erupted, as Steve Flett vainly tried to intervene. "I was having a real go at him. I felt betrayed. He said that he did not realise he could trust me as much as he could. He said, 'I have never lied, Suze, to you because I never did vote you off.' That's a bit like saying to your wife, 'I never slept with her because she was having her period.' It was resolved, finally, and we had a laugh and had a beer. He was very, very apologetic."

After the ordeal they had been through, topped off by that nerve-wracking Tribal Council, both of them felt strange. Staying in a house felt odd; Susannah said she felt the whole place was rocking, like a boat. They consumed endless sandwiches and bottles of beer, staying up until 3am, unable to stop talking. It took a while for them to realise it was over. The next morning after a good scrub they went in to Bocas for a debrief with Steve Flett, before visiting the town's bars for the evening. The next day they were flown to Panama City for the night before travelling back to the UK and their families. Jonny was back at work within a couple of weeks, while Susannah was waiting to see the public fall-out from the TV programme before she started to find another teaching job. Both had their eyes fixed firmly on the final show on 29 May.

Charlotte's Million Year

This is an exclusive interview conducted with last year's *Survivor* winner, Charlotte Hobrough. It took place at the *Survivor Raw* studios in London, shortly after Charlotte had watched the fifth episode of *Survivor 2*.

How has the last year been since you won Survivor?

Hectic but fun.

Has your life changed?

It has definitely changed materially, though personally I haven't changed. I mean, I have a bigger house; a house that I would never, ever have been able to afford in my life with the job I was doing. It has given me more time to spend with Mark and my family because I didn't go back to the police force. I'm on a five-year career break.

Does it feel different, being a millionaire?

Definitely not. We have bought the house outright and a lot of the money has been invested. Of course, we spent money on different things and bought luxury items, like a Jacuzzi, and I've got a few more clothes. But it really doesn't feel any different at all. If I had won, say, £100,000, then I would have blown the lot and carried on working. But because it is a million I have been a bit more sensible. It's not enough to go around living the high life if you want a secure future. This was a one-off for us, so you have to be disciplined. We have bankers who help us, though loads of financial advisers dropped their cards through the door. What was quite funny

was that loads of diamond dealers got in touch because I
mentioned diamonds and how I wanted one. But obviously I
haven't bought one – I've got a fake one (*she laughs*). The
majority of money I gave away to family and friends so they
could buy nice things.

*Obviously there is a positive side to winning a show like this, but
there is a negative side also, such as the press attention. Has that
been easy to cope with?*

At first, all the press was difficult but you reach a stage where
you just don't buy the newspapers any more. What you don't
know doesn't hurt you. My friends and my family don't bother
telling me if there's a bad story in the newspapers. I would
hate to think of it as negative; perhaps I did last year when all
the nasty things came out. But I just think this has not been a
negative thing for me. It has been really positive and it has
only made Mark's life and mine better. Where we live now is a
total dream. You only live once and we have a house on the
beach.

So was it worth it?

Definitely. It's made me more resilient and a much stronger
person. Before *Survivor* I always wanted everyone to like me
and hated any criticism, but that just doesn't happen in life.
There will always be people who don't like you, or criticise
you. Go in for a show like this and some people will like you
and some people will hate you. I have forgotten all the
rubbish, all the negativity that was around last year and I just
see the positive. It has been great fun, all in all.

What is the response you get from the general public?

Generally, people are really nice. Obviously, if you go to a
nightclub you get the odd nasty thing being said. The majority
are nice. I remember when the show was on television and I
was in the gym – it was when I was really upset on the island

– some woman came running up to me and gave me a big hug
and squeezed me really tight. 'Oh you poor thing,' she said,
'we feel so sorry for you.' Some people's reaction was strange.
The children have always been the sweetest. It was really
popular with kids.

What are your impressions of this year's Survivor?
Well, the swearing is worse (*she laughs*). I think I swore twice
under extreme pressure but this lot seem to be at it the whole
time. Meeta swore all the time. I am enjoying it. It's great fun
watching it and not being there.

Would you like to have been there?
No way. It was funny, because it was about this time last year
that I was out there last time and a couple of weeks ago I
knew that was the time when they were filming the new
Survivor. I was waking up in the morning and having my
breakfast, thinking, "They are going to be starving". I'm going
to bed in my lovely, cosy bed and you're thinking about them
sleeping on hard boards and getting about one hour's sleep a
night. It's just going to be hell for them. It's great to watch
other people going through the same thing.
It's different; the contestants are different. I don't know
whether it was because some people were a bit mean on the
show I was on, so people don't want to be perceived as nasty,
like Eve or JJ were perceived as. They are the two names I
always get mentioned to me. People say, "I can't believe you
didn't punch them on the nose" and things like that. But even
though I hated it when I was there with people arguing and
fighting, people I spoke to afterwards said they thought that
made the show in many respects.

What qualities do you need to succeed on Survivor?
You need outright determination. Those people, like Meeta and
Sarah, who said they wanted to go, well that's just ridiculous.
You should not go in for the show unless you are 100 per cent

determined and hell bent on winning. Even though you forget that for a period of time, it comes in to your mind towards the end. If people aren't making alliances then you have to and it doesn't have to be nasty because it's just a game. You don't scream at someone in Monopoly if they buy Park Lane and you wanted it. It's a game and you have to treat it like that.

Have you noticed any differences in this series of Survivor *from the last?*

The weather is horrendous. I feel really sorry for them. The new island they went to for the merger looks an absolute nightmare. They have these horrible biting ants. But they haven't got rats; I would have liked to see someone else eat a rat. It is soaking all the time and they must have been freezing cold. At least we had the heat. Even though that became a pain in itself, I think I would rather be hot than cold. But the food they had to eat in the immunity challenge, the fish eyes and everything, was gross. Apart from the bulls' testicles, which just looked like a piece of meat. But the eye and the crab and the beetle were awful and when it crunched it made me feel sick. That was a harder challenge than we had; we just had to eat one bug.

What are your plans for the future?

I really enjoy TV and so obviously I will keep an open mind about presenting. It's a fantastic position for me to be in because it is such a fickle industry and I've always got the security behind me, so I can try my luck and see what happens. My husband is going to study to be a barrister, so he has the opportunity to do different things. I haven't really planned anything. We have not had any holidays since it happened, so we want to go around Australia before we have children. But who knows what the future holds?

The Last Word

Wednesday 29 May saw the Survivors gather to rubber-stamp Jonny's victory. While it might not have been a foregone conclusion, even Susannah knew her chances of victory were remote at the very best. Despite knowing she would be beaten, and heavily so, the dignified way she accepted defeat won her many admirers, even among those who had previously been fully paid-up members of the anti-Susannah faction. Likewise, Jonny gathered his stunning prize without a hint of arrogance and self-congratulation. His easy charm, quick wit and all-round bonhomie won him all six votes from the jury, including, surprisingly, Bridget, who was much maligned by the Scottish policeman. But he also trounced Susannah in the popular vote. Almost a million and half people called in to register their opinion on the two finalists – including more than a million in one hour – and the result was crushing for Susannah, who garnered just 11 per cent of the votes. A word of warning to any future Survivors: it doesn't pay to be overtly middle class and female, it would seem.

Conversely, it seems to help if you are in the police force.

"Where there's breath, there's hope," was Alastair's phrase on the island. But Susannah was fully aware that her chances were minimal. She was shocked and upset by John's comment when he voted. "I can only believe the money will have a negative effect on you," he told the camera as he held Jonny's name aloft, perhaps bitterness at his own departure at Susannah's hands a factor. John can console himself with the fact that he was many people's favourite, the Dudley Moore for a new generation. Bridget's vote for Jonny followed and Susannah realised then that any hope had been extinguished. With the public vote in the bag, all Jonny required to take the million was the vote of Dave. After saying that Susannah was the "poshest" person he had ever met – "He needs to get out more," she said later – it was obvious where his loyalties lay and Jonny was a millionaire. Given his efforts in the challenges and the way he won over every single person who went on the islands, he was a worthy winner. Upon realising he had won, he let out a huge roar of delight, hugged his girlfriend Ruth and then demolished a plastic crate containing the million pounds – in cash.

After fending off the attentions of Fleet Street's finest – televised live on ITV 2, what did the viewers do to deserve seeing them? – Jonny joined the party. All the Survivors mingled for the first time since coming off the island. Bridget congratulated Jonny, though she found a chance to whisper in his ear, in reference to one of his cattier comments, "Not bad for the most boring woman in the world, eh?" He apologised profusely. Also among the guests were three of last year's Survivors: Charlotte Hobrough, who was presenting ITV 2's *Survivor Raw*, the runner-up Jackie Carey and Andy Fairfield, the favourite of many an English housewife. Jackie, who knows all about losing a final 7-0, offered words of comfort and advice to Susannah. "She put in a sterling effort," she said. "She was so good in all those challenges, far better than me, and I told her I wasn't worthy. It's disappointing to lose like that but she is a very strong woman and she will get over it, I have no doubt about that at all." Spoken by a woman who knows. For those interested, Jackie took last year's final defeat in her stride, still works for British Airways and is "doing very well, thank you."

After being consoled by her family and husband Barney, whom she described as 'a rock', Susannah kindly agreed to be interviewed for the book.

How have the last 12 weeks been?

It's been really hard, a true ordeal. It was a great experience but I am so relieved now it's over. I knew the first two episodes of the series would be bad for me because I cocked up the first immunity challenge and then did the dirty on Lee. I knew it was not going to be positive. But I never expected to encounter such hatred, on the websites and things like that. I have never come across that before in my life and all my family and friends were saying, "This is so unfair. This is so not you." Barney has just been amazing, and he's got upset about so many comments but he's very supportive. A lot of the other contestants were quite guarded and, because they were so "nice," a villain had to be found and I was that villain. I fed the stereotype to an extent but I was just being honest. I think a lot of the others were not honest to the camera.

Did you expect to lose 7-0?

I knew I would lose, even when I took Jonny through

to the final. I might have got more votes with John but I felt more comfortable with Jonny. I liked him more and after what I did to Lee, I did not want to go through that again. I had a secret hope I might get one vote from Bridget, but I think most of the people on the island wanted a male survivor to win. I'm not saying that's bad, I think Jonny's a great guy and if I was not going to win it, he is the only other one I would have wanted to win. But Bridget, I think, felt too close to me as a friend rather than a contender for the million. I have no hard feelings though, juries often vote unanimously and I was guilty of slagging her off a bit, so I'm not too gutted.

Were you the victim of inverted snobbery?

Yes. I think if I had a Scottish accent or a Northern Irish accent then I would never have had half the problems that I had. Dave certainly had a problem with me, and Alastair, well, he's all right actually. I don't think being posh was a problem for him – I just don't think he knew how to take me as a strong woman. There were a lot of things going against me to be honest. All this stuff, "Susannah is really ambitious," and all that is odd. That is seen as negative in relation to me. But if you say about a guy, "Oh, he's really ambitious, he wants to get on in the world," then that's positive. I wanted to keep up with the boys and saw no reason why I should not do as well as they did. I feel massively misunderstood, Dan, I really do. (laughs)

But I do like Dave and Alastair and it's great to see everyone. The one I am angry about is John, because I never said anything nasty about him the whole time I was there and during his last few days on the island he

said some quite nasty things about me. I query his
motives actually. I think he knew I had won the last
immunity challenge and he was confident I might take
him through, so I think he wanted to try and pollute the
public vote as much as possible against me. It's just a
theory but I am a bit bitter now.

*Do you think you could have moderated the things you said,
the way you spoke?*
I was me, to be honest. I don't think you can be
someone else when you spend 24 hours a day with
people. I didn't read Shakespeare as often as it came
across on the TV, only when other contestants asked
me. I could have moderated it a bit, I suppose, but I'm
guilty of telling the truth when someone asks a
question. Jonny was quite clever in the way he chose to
phrase the question about my car. It was not, "What car
have you got?" He knew I didn't have a car; I have a
bike. Instead he asked what car Barney had. He's got a
BMW but it's a company car and it's rented. I'm a
teacher, the idea I'm loaded is bizarre. My Dad is a
solicitor who does some judging part-time. I mean,
John's a barrister, Alastair's an oil baron or something,
Jonny's a detective, they all earn far, far more than me.
Go figure.

Do you have any regrets about the way you played the game?
I regret getting tonsillitis just after we merged because I
really did not feel like speaking to anyone and that was
a time when everyone was getting to know each other,
forming opinions, so that was a blow. I do sort of regret
not owning up to the secret alliance I had with Jonny
earlier because he would have perhaps been seen as the

devious one, apart from me. He's a great guy and he definitely knows what he's doing. He's trained in getting to know people and what they want and how to behave. He is used to taking on personas, but he is also a really personable guy. Saying that, he was definitely more devious than ever came across on the programme.

What now?

I want to get back into a full-time permanent role at a really good school. I have really, really missed teaching over the last few weeks. I gave up my job at a school that I loved and that was difficult. But hopefully there will be a school with an open mind, or that has not watched *Survivor*, to take me on. Thank God for the summer holidays between now and September. I'm hoping they will forget about some of the comments I made, particularly the one about Barney's capacity as a lover. I was watching that beside my Gran and it was hugely embarrassing. "Well dear," she said, "you tried your best and it doesn't matter because you thought you were with friends." I almost died.

Jonny was finding it difficult to get his mind around his achievement. He was walking around in a daze, understandable given the fact he had just become a millionaire. Between interviews for the press and television and the attentions of the huge Scottish contingent that travelled down to London, he answered a few questions.

How does it feel to be a millionaire?

Mental, absolutely mental. It hasn't sunk in yet.

Did you have a good idea you were going to win before the final show was screened?

People kept on saying to me, "You've got it in the bag." I really, honestly, thought "No I haven't". I refused to let myself believe it. Obviously, there were times when I lay in bed thinking about what I would do if I won the million but then I would try to block it out of my mind because otherwise you go mad. If you don't win it, and you let yourself think you have, then you'll be really gutted.

What are you going to do with the money?

I honestly don't know. The main thing is that I will seek financial advice. I would like to buy a house but not before speaking to someone about the best way to use the money. I do fancy an Audi TT or a wee Lotus Elise or something like that. I might be able to spare £25,000 or so for something like that. Definitely a holiday as well: maybe Panama (laughs).

You're not going to take John's advice about getting a new haircut then?

No, not yet. Cheeky b*stard.

Will you keep in touch with any of the Survivors?

Definitely John and definitely Drew, but to be honest I would like to keep in touch with everybody.

Susannah?

Yes, definitely. I like Susannah. She played the game really well and got to the last two. She had one of the best strategies of all the survivors and all her preparation was amazing.

*What about the so-called secret alliance you
had with her?*

We agreed not to vote against each other but I did not
believe her. I just did not trust her. She said she would
not vote against Lee and she did. I might have got her
wrong but there are two schools of thought: that she
took me through, like she says, because I was her best
friend and she got on with me best. But then there is
another school of thought, which friends at work
suggested to me, that says she took me through because
John had more support with the jury and would be far
better at giving a speech because he is a barrister and
he would be much better at answering questions. I
really don't know. I would like to believe it is the first
reason.

But I did help her out. On the Log Stand, when we
were discussing votes after she had got off, Alastair said
his tribe would vote for Susannah because she was a
threat. I could have left it but I decided to fight her
corner and pointed out the effort she put in on the log.
I stuck to the alliance all the way through but I trusted
John far more. To me, he deserved to win it. He is the
ultimate survivor. I would never have voted against him,
even if it meant me losing.

*But at Tribal Council you were asked if your bond
was unbreakable. He said it was and you said it was no
more important than any other alliance. Why?*

There were two reasons for that: firstly, when Mark
asked that I panicked, I thought, "Shit, John might be in
an alliance with someone else and I don't know about
it." I was never 100 per cent certain about John, only 98
per cent, so it crossed my mind there was another

alliance that I knew nothing about. I would have looked
a complete idiot if I had said it was unbreakable and
then he votes me off. That was the main reason. The
other reason was playing the game. I didn't want
Susannah to know about my alliance with John,
or John to know about Susannah. To me, that's part of
the game. Announcing your alliance in a public forum
like Tribal Council is not what the game is all about.

*What do you think the secret of your popularity was, both
with the jury and the viewers?*

I think myself and John had a lot of good banter going
between us. I think that might have appealed to people
at home. Susannah does come across as quite posh;
actually, I wouldn't say she's posh but she's very well-
spoken, everything is said quite dramatically and
enunciated very clearly and that could have annoyed
people.

Did the viewers get to see the real Jonny Gibb?

Not for the first two weeks, because I was very nervous,
fazed by all the cameras, and I found it difficult. It was
my intention to be quite quiet but I did not have to try
given the circumstances. But as time went on I relaxed
more and for the last three weeks what people saw was
the real me.

*But was it the case that people got the impression you were
friends with them when in reality you were slagging them off
behind their back? Like Bridget, for example.*

No, because everyone there I really liked, so it was not
false. I watched the first series and I thought there
would be people like JJ or Eve, awful people who I

could not stand and it would be very difficult to try and
pretend you liked them. I did like everyone, truly and,
yes, I slagged Bridget off loads and loads but it was
quite a stressful situation and you have to vent it
somehow and Bridget copped that. At first some of her
wee stories were quite funny and cute at the beginning
but 24 hours a day, seven days a week, they do begin
to grate on your nerves somewhat. But Bridget is lovely
and I have apologised because I did not want her to get
the impression I hated her. She has been brilliant about
it as well. I do feel guilty because she did not deserve
half the things I said about her. Watching it at home I
was cringing, thinking "I can't believe I said that." I was
obviously more stressed than I thought I was and that
was my reaction.

*How has the last 12 weeks affected your life, your
job in particular?*

Contrary to what was said, I have had no problems with
my work. All the undercover nonsense was blown out
of all proportion. I was plain-clothes but last September
I became a Detective Constable and had to wear a suit
every day. I was not doing surveillance. Every criminal
in the area knows a CID car and when you turn up at
people's door they know you are CID.

There were a few worries about the quotes about
coke and prostitutes but my bosses were willing to wait
and see how it came across on screen and when they
saw it they realised it was all tongue-in-cheek. It's my
sense of humour and people know that. It was strange
working while the show was on. I was in court one
week giving evidence and when I walked out the father
of one of the accused came up to me and rather than

the abuse you often get, he said, "Watched you on the telly mate, you're doing great. Well done," and shook my hand.

I meet my bosses next week to discuss my future. Obviously it is going to be difficult given all the attention I am going to get. I would like to stay but it is going to be very hard.